Courier

CONTENTS

144 WANG & SÖDERSTRÖM

182 SUNNE VOYAGE

32 EL UNION

CONTENTS

242 LA BANCHINA

42 OLO SURF & NATURE

How many times have you got away from the nine to five on a break or holiday only to find your head buzzing with multiple ideas for quitting your job and starting something yourself in an entirely new location? If you're anything like me, you've spent countless hours dreaming up all sorts of beachside, foreign city and mountain-top businesses. It's so easy when you're away from the humdrum to let your mind wander and your imagination fire. But fast-forward to touch down and, within 24 hours of getting home, those dreams begin to fade and are soon forgotten, as life as you previously knew it takes over. In this book, the first of a new series, we're delivering you the antidote to post-holiday amnesia. Inside, you'll find incredible founders from all around the world and their inspiring stories – which constitute just the sort of businesses we've dreamed of owning in the past – alongside a host of factual information to help you take the first step. Of course, we've dispatched our finest photographers to capture them in all their glory. And, if the only thing you do with this book is rest it open on your favorite page to make your home look lovely, you'll get a good return on your investment. But… if you actually use these pages to revive all those dreams you've had in the past and put you in a state where you can sit down, imagine and begin planning to bring something to life… Well, you could reap untold rewards. After all, the old adage is true: life is so much richer if you can spend your Monday to Friday doing something you love. I hope that with this book we can jump-start that kind of shift in your own story.

Until next time,
Jeff Taylor, founder, Courier.

MOND

A micro hotel, surf spot and creative residency.

In 2019, on the southern tip of Sri Lanka, Renato Kümin and Jessica Fernando opened Mond, a six-room micro hotel that they'd spent the previous three years building from the ground up. The couple found the location through a stroke of relative luck on one of their regular trips over from Zurich, where they were living and working at the time. (Jessica's father is from Colombo – she grew up between Sri Lanka and Switzerland.) A keen surfer, Renato was scouting Google Maps when he came across the exact kind of horseshoe-shaped bay that creates the ideal wave formations.

'We drove to this spot based solely on the coordinates,' he remembers. 'It didn't have a name. There wasn't a soul anywhere – nowhere to get coffee or a beer.'

Not that it mattered. Frustrated by the demands of their career-driven city life – they each owned their own business and had backgrounds in branding and communication – the two immediately pictured themselves living on the bay. But the money just wasn't there – until, suddenly, it was. Renato happened to win a new car, a Volvo, in a competition. He immediately sold it to make some fast cash to fund their new project.

The first struggle was purchasing the land. 'There weren't any agents at all, so we had to dig in with the locals,' says Renato. 'We started coming for two months at a time, knocking on doors, spending countless hours at weddings and drinking tea with the nearby families. That's just how you did it and, eventually, we were offered a plot.'

Over celebratory beers back in Zurich with some architect friends, the day-dreaming and planning began. Eight months later, the couple were on a flight, having given up their apartment and careers to spend every day overseeing the construction. Working with local builders and electricians was vital to the couple, who were determined to establish long-term partnerships, down to the fishermen who still supply their restaurant.

'All we did was surf, design, build and learn about construction,' Renato says of their first year living on the island.

The completed Mond, on a cliff overlooking the bay, now stands as a two-floor brutalist concrete structure softened by rounded corners, plenty of wood and tactical holes for ventilation. 'Concrete is a very common material in Switzerland, where we were before. But you don't see it at all in Sri Lanka – which is surprising, because it's so suitable for the tropical environment. We wanted to soften the brutality of the material, to create the organic shapes that you see throughout the hotel. That's why we have so many round openings, round walls.'

While the pandemic and Sri Lanka's ongoing economic crisis have certainly served up challenges, a typical day for the couple and their daughter still involves 'a lot of beach time', including 'at least two or three swims per day'. And, recently, as the business has grown and they've hired more staff, Renato says that he and Jessica have 'finally started surfing together again as a date activity', just like they did on their very first visit.

Renato and Jessica
live in a house less than
a minute's walk away from
the hotel. In 2020, they
welcomed a daughter, Ru,
who's now 'basically a part
of the business. We don't
have nannies, grandparents
around or daycare, so
she's always around and
guests get to know her.'

Once the basic structure of the hotel was in place, the couple's creative friends came to join them for three-month 'mini residencies', helping to design the furniture and ceramics that now make up the decor.

The hotel's remote location meant that final touches took a while. 'Just being out here was our main challenge,' Renato says. 'We ended up designing a lot of custom pieces that we didn't expect, from lamps to handles, locks [and] sliding mechanisms for doors, all by ourselves, because we couldn't find them nearby.'

'We ended up designing a lot of custom pieces that we didn't expect.'

Alongside surf lessons, guests can also enjoy calligraphy workshops, courtyard musical performances and talks, and regular 'clay dates', where they can spend an afternoon throwing clay with Jessica, who's a ceramicist in her free time. The couple plan to open Studio Mond in the near future, which will sell many of the functional products they've designed for the property. 'Guests are always asking whether they can buy stuff from the hotel [that we've designed] –

people want to be able to take a bit of Mond home with them,' says Renato. 'We're in the early days of establishing an artists' residency as well – we've had different artists in residence and talks, which we want to keep growing.'

Food and beverage offerings include brunch at the cafe six days a week, with cocktails and sharing plates in the bar at night. Each year, a new chef flies in to refresh the menus and train the in-house cooks.

'You have to be in love enough with what you do to roll with the punches.'

'You have to be in love enough with what you do to roll with the punches,' insists Renato, when asked to reflect on the fact that their wild bet has paid off. 'It's not easy, but that's what life is for. Give it a go and, as long as no one dies, it's fine. You can always go back to what you had before.

'You try to create this beautiful space that people can come and enjoy, and there's a lot of pressure on the hotel to create that magic. We realized that guests also have to come with the right mindset, because everyone contributes to that experience. We end up becoming friends with 95% of the guests. That's the magic of having only six rooms and being a small business.

'But it's also work – it can get exhausting when you're open for seven days a week, 24 hours a day, for six months straight. We need to try to find a balance. We need to put structures in place and have the right staff to enable us to step back sometimes.'

CLÉMENT BOUTEILLE FLEURS

A seasonal flower farmer, florist and seed forager.

Raised in the French countryside, Clément Bouteille has never been too far removed from nature. For generations, his family have spent their lives maintaining a farm in the former commune of Saint-Maurice-sur-Dargoire (now part of Chabanière), outside Lyon, harvesting fresh fruits and vegetables, grapes for wine and medicinal herbs like rosemary, chamomile and echinacea.

In 2019, Clément, who's now in his late 20s, returned home after working in Belgium and, ever since, the farm has been home to Clément Bouteille Fleurs, a busy florist and plant nursery serving customers all across France.

As a teenager, while he developed his interest in plants and flowers, Clément studied landscape design. He then enrolled in art school in Paris, after which he jumped between jobs in the fashion industry. But he wasn't quite satisfied with a career in clothes and dreamed of having a job that was more 'connected to nature', he says.

Things began to change in 2018, after he took a trip to explore the wildlife of French Guiana. Inspired by the plants that he'd seen, Clément reached out to floral designer Mark Colle. 'Floristry seemed like a really good mix between creativity, having clients and discussing projects with people, and the nature part and the plant knowledge,' Clément explains. Later that year, Mark invited Clément to his studio and shop, Baltimore Bloemen, in Antwerp to learn the ropes of the floristry trade. Clément Bouteille Fleurs was conceived around a year later.

Whereas many traditional florists offer the same range of popular flowers and plants all year round, Clément specializes in unusual and rare botanical varieties and grows them only when they're in season. For this reason, you won't find any heated greenhouses on the farm.

Clément couldn't find many of his favorite flowers at flower markets, which tend to sell the same easy-to-grow blooms almost year-round. 'I wanted to bring a better connection to sustainability and the seasons,' he says. For similar reasons, he keeps his flower arrangements free from plastic. And, because he sells his cut flowers locally, they're often picked only a few hours before they arrive with the customer – helping to retain the flowers' fragrance.

Today, Clément Bouteille Fleurs offers an ever-changing assortment of perennial plants, as well as dried flowers and ornamental vegetables. But its real specialty is its range of freshly grown flowers. To source them, Clément often scours the internet looking for old seed catalogs, which he'll then nurture on the farm. 'Sometimes there are varieties that are really cool, but you have to really dig on the internet to find them,' he says. He avoids buying from any companies that sell genetically modified seeds.

On a deeper level, the business was about giving Clément freedom to live and work on his own terms. 'Ever since I was a child, when I heard two adults talking about how they were waiting for holidays, I knew I didn't want to spend my life that way,' he says.

Clément first became interested in plants and flowers through butterflies and tropical insects, which he spent a large chunk of his childhood breeding. 'When you want to raise many kinds of insects, you have to build a plant collection,' he says.

When he's not traveling, he'll often spend days in the countryside foraging for seeds, which he'll then take back to the farm. 'Some seeds are so complicated to find that you can't find them on the internet,' he says. 'You have to go out in the wild.'

Clément's commitment to seasonality and protecting the environment does mean that from December to April, when the weather is cooler, he has very few flowers. But, during this time, he sells foliage and blossom branches, teaches in a horticultural school and consults for an architecture firm to help source the right kinds of plants for its buildings.

'You can't find them on the internet. You have to go out in the wild.'

'I have no days that look the same and that's something I've always been into.'

Clément has recently hired his first employee and hopes to open up a garden in southern France, where he'll be able to grow tropical plants that'll bloom in winter.

'I have no days that look the same and that's something I've always been into,' he says.

To pay for his investment in rare seeds, Clément sells flowers individually to florists and private customers.

He creates unique flower arrangements that he presents at fashion shows and events.

In his arrangements, Clément loves to incorporate wildflowers and plants that he's plucked from nature during one of his many foraging trips. 'A lot of people dismiss them, but I love to find ways to present them as beautiful – because that's what they are,' he says. 'Sometimes you just need to change the context around them to change the view.'

As well as working with Mark Colle, Clément developed his skills with Parisian florists Debeaulieu and Castor Fleuriste.

EL
UNION

A beachside coffee bar and roastery with a skate park.

Since opening in 2013 in San Juan, La Union, on the north-west coast of the Philippines, El Union Coffee has grown from a simple coffee shack to a community hub complete with a skating bowl and bean roastery. Situated right next to the beach, it's not hard to see why founders Kiddo and Amy Cosio decided to move here from Manila more than a decade ago.

'[We] were 20-something newlyweds growing increasingly dissatisfied with life in a massive city,' says Kiddo. 'While we love our hometown, it is one of the most congested cities on the planet and, like most Manila folk, I was spending at least 20 hours a week on my work commute.'

When the couple first moved to La Union, it was still a quiet surf town. But in the years since, it's become a booming tourist destination for locals and foreigners alike. Kiddo says that the initial goal was to 'serve a few great coffees to a sleepy neighborhood while funding a simple life at the beach'.

Originally they opened a 'parking-space sized' coffee shack but, as Kiddo says, 'Our business has grown alongside the growth of the town. Aside from a cafe, we now have a small roastery that delivers coffee beans nationwide, a lab, a cocktail bar called The Shrine of Satisfaction, and an office team. We're working toward setting up a farm, mill and coffee-buying station in the near future.'

Commitment to sourcing the best beans is key to the couple's success. 'We source most of our coffees from northern Philippine specialty coffee farmers and producers, with whom we trade directly. We pride ourselves [on] our transparent and direct trade with coffee-farming communities,' says Kiddo. The Philippines might not have an international reputation of coffee culture, but it's a thriving industry. 'I wish more privileged folk understood that there's more to speciality coffee than cup scores. Our company is out to positively impact how Filipinos eat, drink, and live.'

The quality of the food and coffee is what has cemented El Union's reputation: it serves chocolate cornflake cookies alongside the extensive coffee menu and house-made spiced chai blend, and bakes milk bread daily on-site for its famous grilled-cheese sandwiches and horchata-soaked French toast with pandan custard. When demand for the brand took off, Kiddo and Amy launched an online store where they sell beans, blends and merch. A recent collaboration with Filipino heritage brand Islander saw profits go to El Union's Farmer Fund, which assists small-hold coffee farming communities.

Community is a crucial part of the business – El Union sponsors the town's sports teams and local LGBTQ+ events, and pays its staff on average 30% more than local industry standards. For Kiddo, the best part of running the day-to-day of a busy coffee shop is the employees: 'Our slogan, "Coffee in the service of humans" is a mantra to inform everything from labor philosophy [and] sourcing protocol to creative strategy [and] business development. I love our team, including our alumni, some of whom are now coffee entrepreneurs on their own.'

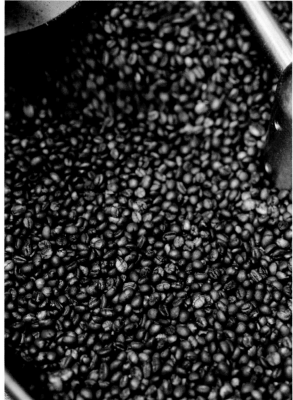

Coffee is at the heart of what El Union is and has always been Kiddo and Amy's focus. No matter if it's their caffeinated take on the Mexican drink horchata (their best-selling coffee on the menu) or the bag of blended espresso beans or bottles of cold brew they sell in the cafe, supporting the community that exists around coffee is key.

'I wish more global north communities would give weight to global south perspectives when it comes to food and drink; after all, many ingredients, like coffee, only grow in the tropics, and most producing countries are underdeveloped, extracted from, and often colonized by the richer societies,' says Kiddo.

It's something that they want people to be able to take away from their time at El Union and recreate at home. So much so that Amy recently shared her now not-so-secret recipe for their horchata on their website.

'Our company is out to positively impact how Filipinos eat, drink, and live.'

As El Union grows, Kiddo and Amy want to become even more involved in the ways that their business can support the coffee industry at home in the Philippines as well as abroad. 'We envision being more involved in farming and processing coffee here in the Philippines – it's a vehicle for the social progress of underprivileged farmers,' Kiddo says.

'We're already doing the field work to prepare for a milling and processing center for coffee and other companion crops. Ultimately, we'd love to grow our own coffee.'

'Our name is a jab at colonialism: the Philippines was colonized by Spain for hundreds of years, and later, by the US. Our misgendered "El Union" [correct Spanish grammar is "La Union"] is a tiny assertion of our own voice as a people that have been severely exploited and extracted from. It also expresses our love for La Union, our province. The name is saying: it's our turn to speak, please listen.'

OLO SURF & NATURE

A sustainability-focused surf school and guesthouse.

During the long months that Amine Lamriki would spend in the desert near the city of Ouarzazate during his career in the Moroccan film industry, all that he could think about was located just a few hours away: the surf hitting Morocco's Atlantic coast. 'I used to drive six hours to Taghazout to try to get two waves on a Sunday,' he says, 'only to drive back by the evening and, at 4am, start shooting again.'

It wasn't necessarily that he didn't love his job. He quit school at 15 to join Morocco's fast-growing film industry (the country has been the backdrop to movies like Prince of Persia: The Sands of Time and TV series like Game of Thrones) and worked his way up from an assistant to running sets. But after 20 years of grueling projects – some with 16-hour days, stretched across 10 months – it was either move up the career ladder or take a chance on building something from his passion for surfing.

So, Olo Surf & Nature, his surf school and accommodation business, was born. First, he had to find the right location. Nearby towns like Taghazout felt too built up. He thought of a small fishing village, Imsouane, set well off the main highway, perched on a cliff between two renowned surf spots: Cathedral, with reliable left and right breaks (the direction that a wave's peak moves), and Magic Bay, with a mythical right break that stretches 700 meters (roughly a two-minute ride) on its best days.

He'd been coming to the spot since it was really undiscovered, camping or renting cheap rooms with few amenities. 'It was so random and empty, and I really fell in love with it,' he says. Over time, it had become a destination for tourists and Moroccans seeking the country's best surf. So, he rented a house to see if he could create a business where people could stay, surf and see what he'd fallen in love with. His first guesthouse quickly booked up.

While many hotels along Morocco's coast were built and are run with little regard to the natural environment, Amine has kept sustainability at the core of Olo. His team compost waste, grow their own herbs and vegetables, source products from local farmers, collect rainwater for watering plants and produce their own environmentally friendly shampoos and soaps.

That said, it hasn't always been as blissful as a surf in the sun. When Morocco closed its borders as the pandemic hit, the business had to be pared back to survive – Amine refocused on delivering a quality experience to those who *were* able to visit. Now, his expansion efforts are based on connecting with surf and nature enthusiasts, not just holidaymakers – he recently opened a surf shop with specialty boards and has plans to build off-grid accommodation in a remote spot further along the coast.

'We work hard, that's for sure. But we work in an environment where people are happy – you see the waves, and you go and share two hours surfing with your friends and guests. That's why I'm here,' he says, before adding: 'I can now check the surf from my bed. It's life-changing.'

As surfing has become more popular – and people have become more willing to travel further to find a wave – many surf towns have become overcrowded and built up. Just down the coast from Imsouane, Taghazout is packed with resorts.

Benefiting from being far away from the main highway, Imsouane has maintained more of a community feel. 'It's all small businesses everywhere. It stays quite human-sized,' says Amine.

This may change as new developments are on the horizon. But any expansion for Olo will be rooted in ecological awareness and keeping this human-sized mentality, building on the sustainability practices that Amine has already developed.

'It's all small businesses everywhere. It stays quite human-sized.'

Going from running movie sets to running surf camps was something of a learning curve. Initially, Amine *(right)* thought he'd base himself in Imsouane and go back to Ouarzazate if a film project came up. Olo was a far cry from the movie stars and fancy sets he worked on in his previous career.

'I'd never had to serve breakfast for people at six in the morning so they could get ready to surf,' he laughs.

But he was hooked. 'It was very challenging and exciting to learn new things and develop the business.'

Olo's villas, perched along Imsouane's cliffs, are designed to be calming and welcoming so that people truly feel at home – with thoughtfully decorated communal spaces and luxury amenities like a built-in pool and terraces overlooking the bay below. Amine wanted

to recreate the feelings of hospitality that he'd experienced on surf trips around the world.

'I wanted to show people what I had enjoyed in my travels – why did I choose to stay in that guesthouse in Indonesia for three months? Because I felt something special. I tried to recreate this experience with Moroccan specificity, as Morocco is known to be warm and welcoming.'

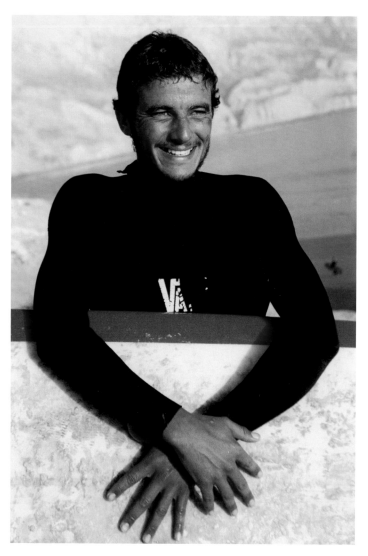

It takes a village to run Olo – Amine has a staff of 30 who are a combination of local Berber villagers, Moroccan surf enthusiasts and people who've traveled from around the world to set up in Imsouane. That said, Amine says that no matter who he's hiring, they need to have an exceptionally welcoming and thoughtful disposition.

'The most important thing is the staff,' he says. 'Without staff that embrace your mentality, you won't be able to do this. They are your voice.'

The sense of hospitality and friendly nature of his staff are what set his business apart, he says. 'We've managed to create an environment that's very welcoming and peaceful, where everyone feels at home and wants to come back. The first people who booked Olo are still coming back now.'

'It was never an option to just do the guesthouse, not including the surf,' says Amine. 'The bay is one of the best spots to learn surfing. We can guarantee to almost anyone that they'll get the longest wave of their life. It's something we wanted to share with people from the very first day.'

That means Olo had to be a multifaceted business. There's a surf school where people can take lessons or attend up to week-long surf camps, with yoga and video analysis. The team also host workshops on environmental awareness in local schools, with an eye to keeping Imsouane's natural beauty intact for the future.

Most recently, Amine opened up his collection of specialty boards for enthusiasts who are looking to try out something new – sometimes he'll bring a selection down to the beach to let people try them out.

'I love to see what works in one condition – why should I use a single fin instead of a thruster?' he says. 'I want people to try all the boards. You can take it out to surf two waves and come back and try something new.'

LAURENCE AIRLINE

A fashion brand and creative community — with a pool.

Turning points don't come much bigger. In 2015, Laurence Chauvin-Buthaud was running her brand Laurenceairline between Abidjan in the Ivory Coast and Paris in France. Then her headquarters caught fire. The blaze was serious – burning down her workshop almost entirely. And yet, to her surprise, 'the fire saved the company'. In a way, she continues, 'the process gave me the opportunity to turn tough experiences into beauty'.

Raised between the Ivory Coast and France, Laurence started her career working at a big luxury fashion brand. Soon, however, she realized she wanted to channel her creativity into her own work. She spent a few years learning the ropes of fashion production as well as designing womenswear and stage costumes, once for Nigerian singer-songwriter Keziah Jones. But it was her first menswear collection – tailored shirts made of African textiles, released in 2010 – when she hit her stride.

'When I was starting my brand, it wasn't trendy to make African fashion,' she says. 'All the raw material was coming from Africa but was transformed outside Africa.' She wanted to integrate local culture into her finished products, ensuring they weren't viewed as seasonal or cliché. Her designs, she explains, 'are really African, [as well as] modern and well-made'.

Growing the brand with stockists all around the world took a personal toll. 'When I finished a collection, I was buying, producing, delivering. I was always executing,' she says. 'After five years, I was totally burned out. And then my factory burned.'

Laurence took it as an opportunity to reset the balance of the brand – and her life. She found a house in Grand-Bassam – a quiet seaside city about an hour and a half from Abidjan – and pared back the business. She kept on seven employees, moved her workshop into the garage, stopped releasing seasonal collections and focused on sustainable materials and unisex designs.

The story of those who make each collection is a central part of how she sells her work – each garment is accompanied by a message from one of her team of master tailors. 'I make my customers understand why I create,' she says.

Now, Laurence's days are less about the grind and more about mindfulness. She calls the new iteration of her brand a 'creative ashram' – a holistic approach to building a business and life that puts care for the community ahead of production goals. 'To help people feel good is the base.'

Her slower approach isn't limiting the company's growth. She's turned part of the house into a boutique, gallery and hang-out space for the local community and visiting artists, and artist residencies and travel retreats are in the works.

Thinking beyond fashion – and imagining how a business can give back – is Laurence's focus moving forward. 'It's been a constant evolution, to be present to hear the needs of my community, the needs of those I'm working with, the needs of my clients, and to create something that resonates with the needs of the planet,' she says. 'For me, my creativity is connected to everything.'

Laurence's base in Grand-Bassam mixes her personal and professional lives. But keeping everything in one place allows her to attend to the daily needs of the business – managing finances and tracking production – while balancing her creative practice, such as dreaming up new projects and taking time for meditation.

'In one space, I have my personal apartment; downstairs, I have the boutique atelier; in another space, there's a workshop; in another space, there's an apartment for people in the arts residency or who've come to work,' she says. 'It's a space where we work all together, but there's space where everyone can breathe and have a personal life.'

With this in mind, she designed the boutique less around making sales and more around sharing space.

'I took time to create this – it's not a supermarket,' she says. 'If you come to visit the space, take off your shoes, let's share a proper moment. Time is so precious – it's the only thing we'll never get back. Let's give value to the time we share.'

'I didn't see
myself in
my business.
I wanted
to be more
in my
feminine
energy.'

After the fire in Laurence's
factory, she had time to
slow down and learned an
important lesson – as well
as set herself a challenge.
'I realized it's not just about
doing things to do things
– I didn't see myself [in my
business],' she says. 'Could
I share something from
a space where I felt good
in myself? I wanted to be
more in my feminine energy.'
From there, she focused
on creating a more holistic
business, with thoughtfully
produced designs alongside
workshops and retreats.

'If you do something where you put in care and love, it's powerful.'

The wider fashion world quickly took to Laurence's unique vision of combining African fabrics and craftsmanship with western tailoring. But, these days, she's focused more on staying true to the internal team that's driven the brand forward.

'More than a brand, I'm a creative and, if I continue to do fashion, it's not because I love fashion – it's because I built a story with my team,' she says. 'Some of the people I work with, we've known each other for more than 20 years – it's a life story.'

Her clothing collections have been inspired by this community, particularly growing up in West Africa in the eighties. Her material choices are also increasingly shaped by sustainability and the desire to keep production local: 80% of materials in her most recent collection were handwoven by a community of craftspeople in Burkina Faso and dyed using natural pigments.

'I'd like to do clothes that are made with care and love – if you do something where you put in care and love, it's powerful,' she says.

After three years of hosting her workshop in her garage, Laurence was able to buy a portion of the house she lives in – which she has transformed into a public-facing boutique and gathering space for the brand. 'I dreamed of a small garden – a small paradise where people can come and recharge,' she says.

While Grand-Bassam may not garner as much attention as major art hubs like Paris (where she also launched a store this year), opening the doors to the boutique has created a gathering space for the local and international arts community.

'We're creating a sense of destination – if you come to visit one artist, you can visit another,' Laurence says. 'During the weekend, people like to come here – they appreciate having the chance to see something unexpected and discover something beautiful but connected with an experience.'

Laurence has found that basing her brand in the Ivory Coast has helped to surround her with people who find inspiration globally. 'Grand-Bassam has something that's local and international – touching people who like the slow life but want to be connected to the world.'

DREAM BUSINESSES

So, what even is a dream business? We ask some people living and working on their own terms what the phrase means to them

Edson Sabajo *(left)* and Guillaume 'Gee' Schmidt *(right)* are the co-founders of Dutch brand Patta.

Timothy:

'Once you can make your hobby into a business, that's cool, because then it doesn't feel like work any more. [That's] basically what Patta is. It's a nice hobby that's spiraled way out of control. But there's not really one thing that I'm very amazed by, to be honest. Yeah, it's nice working with big brands; it's nice – don't get me wrong – to do collabs. It's dope to make our own product and it's dope to make a [Nike] Air Max or whatever – with one, we make money, with the other, we all make money. But what's the most amazing thing? To be able to build growth, so that people appreciate what we do. It's not based solely on money, but also on the community and the culture we've created. Building together with a community is the greatest thing we do. I'm prouder of the Patta Foundation [a social initiative for minority and young people] than I am of Patta. When we started Patta, it was just a label. We didn't plan it, it just grew. From there, opportunities came. Now we have the Patta Running Team, Patta Cycling [Team], a Patta football school. These are all things where we can rep the community and try to make a difference.'

(SIX)

PATTA

Timothy Sabajo
Amsterdam

In 2004, six months after the first Patta store opened in Amsterdam, the Netherlands, Timothy Sabajo got a call from his brother, Edson, who'd just started the company with Guillaume 'Gee' Schmidt. The call went something like: 'Bro, I want you on board.' Timothy hasn't looked back since. Today, Patta is a major streetwear brand with stores and stockists around the world.

CASA ETÉREA

An off-grid, mirrored guesthouse on an extinct volcano.

A photographer and writer who grew up in Singapore, Prashant Ashoka hit upon his dream business idea almost by chance. On the slopes of an extinct volcano, called Palo Huérfano, in the Los Picachos highlands, near the Mexican city of San Miguel de Allende, Prashant found the land that he'd end up building Casa Etérea on while hiking with a friend in 2017. Surrounded by 10,000 hectares of rugged nature, the mountains' peaks rise up to 2,600 meters in altitude.

'It was land that nobody wanted to buy,' says Prashant. 'There was no road access. No water. No electricity. It was on a 45-degree incline. You can't really use the land for agricultural purposes and it was really difficult [terrain] to build on.'

Even so, he continues, 'I was very moved when I stood on the plot of land for the first time. Everything was in bloom and it was really green. I knew it was the kind of landscape I wanted to build a house on.'

Today, Casa Etérea stands as a super-sleek, one-bedroom house whose shell is largely made from mirrored glass. This mirrored glass, Prashant proudly explains, not only gives guests a 'heightened awareness of their surroundings' but is also bird-friendly, thanks to its ultra-violet coating 'that makes it visible to birds while remaining naked to the human eye'. Casa Etérea's website describes the project as 'livable installation art that uses mirrored panels to diffuse the boundaries between the wild and the structured'.

When it comes to sustainability, no stone has been left unturned. The guesthouse runs on solar energy and harvested rainwater, and is designed to be self-sufficient and in harmony with its surroundings. The foundation is constructed from lava rock, all hand-collected from the volcano on whose slope it sits. Everything was constructed without hiring an architectural firm and by consulting only local carpenters and engineers.

The interior space was designed without partition walls, making the entire house one room. Overlooking a ravine, even the exposed glass shower has great views. From the central living space and bedroom, floor-to-ceiling sliding glass doors frame the huge cliffs, while opening to connect with a decked patio area and a solar-heated pool shaded by olive and pomegranate trees.

Guests can enjoy bespoke adventures led by local residents, including horse riding or hikes with a botanist. But, ultimately, Casa Etérea is pretty isolated. As such, the business offers a free shuttle service to the city when guests arrive and depart – due to the rocky road leading to the house, only SUVs or 4x4s can manage the journey. As more travelers seek out remote experiences, spaces can evolve in order to inspire a deeper examination of our relationship with nature. But, for those guests who really want it, Casa Etérea does offer wifi and a laptop-friendly workspace.

'Sitting here, you can see the passage of time: watch the clouds move by and the house almost seems like it's moving. I like that visual element,' says Prashant. 'Casa Etérea is a theater to nature.'

'Had I known the full scale of the project, I'd have felt ill-equipped to deal with it.'

Prashant was just 28 when he started work on Casa Etérea. 'I didn't understand the scale of the project or the skills or technicality it'd take to accomplish it. I learned along the way. I was blissfully unaware.

'In hindsight, maybe that was a good thing. Because had I known the full scale of the project, I'd have felt ill-equipped to deal with it.

'But you have to go through the motions and work with what you've got, do the best research you can and speak to the right people. I was able to do all those things.'

Local residents like Concho Sierra Mendoza *(right)* are happy to welcome guests *(above)* to Casa Etérea, taking them on trips into the mountains and helping out with house maintenance.

It took nearly three years for Prashant to complete the whole project. 'I just knew it was the right time to do it,' he says, despite 'stumbling' into architecture and having no formal training. 'I knew I just wanted to share this piece of land with more people.'

'Emotional architecture is architecture that moves you and changes how you view your surroundings.'

Conscious of the increasingly digital world we live in and the isolation that can come with it, in recent years architects and designers have been looking to create more spiritually uplifting spaces. Prashant points out that they're all, in some ways, playing off the term 'emotional architecture', which Mexican architect Luis Barragán and sculptor-painter Mathias Goeritz came up with in 1954.

'Emotional architecture is architecture that moves you and changes how you view your surroundings,' he says. 'It's what I'm aiming for. So, for example, I've used the interplay between light and shadows with the use of the mirror.'

PNY

A burger- and design-focused restaurant group.

At the end of his graduate business degree, Rudy Guénaire embarked on a soul-searching adventure across the US instead of joining the corporate rat race. Over four and a half months, he walked alone across the Continental Divide of the Americas – a grueling hiking trail that snakes cross-country between the Mexican and Canadian borders – surviving on just plain tortillas until he reached the nearest town.

'I'd walk for 10 days at a time and then would arrive at these small-town American diners,' Rudy remembers. 'I don't know if the burgers they served were actually that good, but I'd be so famished that they tasted incredible.'

When he returned to Paris, he found himself missing the simple comforts of the all-American diner – as well as its signature dish, the hamburger. So, in 2011, he partnered with former classmate Graffi Rathamohan to launch PNY (an acronym for Paris New York).

With Graffi in charge of food and Rudy responsible for the design, the pair looked to persuade the discerning Parisian dining scene that a burger could be so much more than a cheap, low-quality American export à la McDonald's.

Although it wasn't common to hire an architect to outfit a Parisian restaurant, Rudy knew that to successfully elevate burgers in the eyes of locals, PNY needed the kind of design that would match the high quality of the produce. For the brand's first outpost on Paris' Rue du Faubourg Saint-Denis, Rudy enlisted the expertise of up-and-coming firm Cut Architectures and, together, they designed the restaurant, blending elements of New York and Paris' cultures.

Since then, PNY has expanded into a restaurant group and, today, there are eight sites in Paris and a further six across France, each with unique interiors. After working with Cut Architectures and then Belgian architect Bernard Dubois, Rudy decided to take the reins and start his own design agency, Night Flight.

'I've never studied architecture, but I've done so many site visits and spent so much time around architects,' he explains. 'It happened very naturally, as it's something I'm incredibly passionate about.' A self-confessed literature and film buff (Rudy personally writes the weekly PNY newsletter), he steered clear of Instagram and Pinterest during the conception phase, instead mining his imagination for inspiration. No detail was overlooked – even the napkin holders and beer taps are custom designed by Rudy.

As PNY continues to expand across France, Rudy is mindful of preserving the soul of the business. Each of the brand's restaurants adheres to the strict protocol of French environmental agency Écotable to ensure that both its service and produce are sustainable and environmentally responsible. To do so, it relies on a carefully vetted network of the country's top farmers to supply only the highest-quality produce.

And, as for the unique aesthetics, 'Nothing is done just for the sake of it,' says Rudy. 'Everything has reason and is part of a larger story.'

Within each of PNY's restaurants, references to the classic American diner are weaved into a larger design narrative of cinema, Americana and the history of the city where the outpost is located. The design of every site is bespoke – Rudy creates a unique chair and lamp for each space to match the theme.

Rudy worked with architect Bernard Dubois on three PNY restaurants, including the second outpost in the Parisian district of Le Marais, on Rue Sainte-Croix de la Bretonnerie (above).

Rudy says: 'When I design my restaurants, they're designed with the intention to last at least 20 years,' both in terms of materials and concept.

PNY's cheese is a blend of aged cheddar that's melted until it's a pourable consistency. It's become a signature of the PNY menu.

'It's only natural that our restaurants are more sophisticated than an average American diner.'

'Our job is to celebrate the burger,' explains Rudy. 'So it's only natural that our restaurants are more sophisticated than [an] average [American] diner.'

The menu features everything you'd expect at a classic American diner. But PNY puts its own spin on things, with the fries covered in an 18-month-aged cheddar, the milkshakes featuring Madagascan vanilla and a giant profiterole filled with praline and chantilly cream.

Although the menu is similar at each location, some die-hard fans have made it a challenge to visit each of the restaurants and be photographed in the unique interiors.

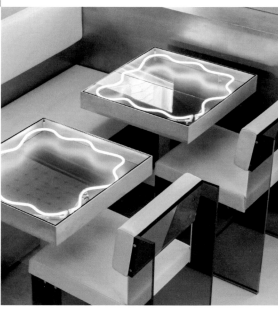

For PNY Lyon, the first restaurant designed entirely by Rudy, he turned to the glamor of Hollywood for inspiration. Ultrafragolas, a type of mirror by designer Ettore Sottsass, hang on shiny midnight-blue lacquered walls, while the tables are gently backlit by neon lights so that 'everyone looks beautiful as they eat'.

The PNY site in the city of Grenoble was designed to look like an airplane interior. Some of the giant concrete windows – inspired by American architect John Lautner – open onto the kitchen and bar, while others are backed by gently pleated Japanese paper. Just like in an airplane, Rudy ensured that no view is the same.

'Nothing is done just for the sake of it – everything has reason and is part of a larger story.'

PNY Strasbourg resembles a fantasy train wagon as imagined through the cinematic gaze of Hong Kong director Wong Kar-wai– a nod to the fact that Strasbourg was historically the first stop on the Orient Express train journey and that the first American diners were styled as mobile dining wagons.

CAMP YOSHI

A collective creating space for people of color in the wilderness.

When Rashad Frazier went camping in Montana's Glacier National Park with his wife, Shequeita, and his brother, Ron, in 2020, not a single part of him expected to return with a new career. A trained chef residing in New York who was out of work because of the pandemic, he simply wanted to spend some quality time with his loved ones. 'At the beginning, it was like: let's just launch this thing and see where it goes,' he recalls. 'Hopefully it'll buy us some time before we go back to our regular jobs.'

Needless to say, he never went back. His idea was Camp Yoshi, a platform for black people and their allies to unplug and reconnect in nature. In practice, this means that Rashad designs and curates camping trips across the US and increasingly further afield.

At its core, Camp Yoshi is an antidote to troubled times. Besides the pandemic, in 2020 there were the deaths of George Floyd, Tony McDade and Breonna Taylor, among countless others, which highlighted racial injustices. 'That summer was so emotionally exhausting, constantly being reminded that we have so much further to go with humanity,' Rashad remembers. Positioned around the campfire in Montana, it struck him that one of the only places he felt truly comfortable was in nature. Why not invite others, so they can be empowered, too?

'Most of my friends come from hyper-urban environments where they're constantly reminded by the television, their peers, newspapers, the media, that the world is broken,' says Rashad.

'I thought our camping trips would be a way to completely digitally detach and be around great folks.'

To launch the company, Rashad turned to his black book. Growing up in South Carolina, he and Ron spent much of their lives exploring the wild together. They'd archived their favorite campsites, routes and hidden treasures, which gave them a company framework. 'We went into the business having all the intel and the routes already locked in,' says Rashad.

In the summer of 2020, he picked out one of his favorite locations, the Alvord Desert in south-eastern Oregon, for the first Camp Yoshi trip. He dissolved Yoshi Jenkins, a boutique Afro-Asian catering company he'd been running, and sent out an email to his contacts inviting them along. With a menu designed by the Yoshi Jenkins team, the trip was an instant success. 'We had over 50 people want to come and we had to narrow it down to 12,' he says.

In 2021 and 2022, Camp Yoshi held dozens more trips, going as far as Mexico and Tanzania and welcoming guests from all around the world. Fast-forward to today and Camp Yoshi runs around 25 trips a year. Rashad limits the number to 'protect the magic of the brand', he says.

In the next few years, Rashad wants to open up his own campsites across the US, allowing more people to experience Camp Yoshi. He also has his eye on more overseas adventures. 'The trips aren't going to be a solution to our problems,' he says. 'They're more about saying: let's give you four, five days of a true disconnect from the world.'

When he first came up with the idea for Camp Yoshi, it was clear to Rashad that there was nothing else like it on the market. Most of the adventure companies targeted at the BIPOC community were non-profits with a social agenda. 'Nobody was really saying: "We know you lot are all out there exhausted from having to wear multiple personalities,"' Rashad says.

He wanted his company to speak to black people in a way that feels 'aspirational and bucket-list-worthy', he says, providing top-of-the-range equipment, delicious food and thrilling experiences.

While Rashad is the face of the business, Ron, a lawyer, works on the business side and Shequeita works on strategy. 'If Rashad is the kite in the sky, the face of all of it, I'm holding the string to the kite and Shequeita is the wind blowing us in any direction,' Ron says. Recently, as the brand has expanded, it's employed two more full-time staff alongside the founding trio.

'It's essentially a three- or four-day camping experience with a bunch of hospitality professionals.'

From the menus and cooking workshops to the water sports and campfires, everything Camp Yoshi does is geared towards making the outdoors more inclusive and creating a 'sense of community and nourishment' in the remote wilderness, says Rashad.

Each trip caters to 15 people, at a cost of around $3,000 to $10,000 each, depending on the location. In return, Camp Yoshi organizes everything from the tents, vehicles, equipment and gear to the activities, which can include rafting, kayaking, hiking and tie-dyeing classes.

Then there's the food and drink: 'Imagine having a full day of adventure and then having an evening eating short ribs or having a whole butterflied grilled rainbow trout with pickled onions,' Rashad says. 'It's essentially a three- or four-day camping experience with a bunch of hospitality professionals.'

CITIZEN OF NOWHERE

A concept store and tea room that celebrates local craftsmanship.

From glassware and sticky-rice baskets to chairs and other furniture, Citizen of Nowhere, a concept store in Bangkok, Thailand, casts its net far and wide. Kitschy, eclectically bold designs unite its range of products. Everything is overseen by founder Saran Yen Panya, a creative director who was born locally and earned a master's degree in storytelling in Stockholm, Sweden.

For nearly a decade, Saran filled his time with 56thStudio, a multidisciplinary design house he founded – but that was before he came up with the concept for Citizen of Nowhere.

Founded in 2018, Citizen of Nowhere exists to build awareness of Thailand's craftspeople, whose reach can be limited by technological barriers. It focuses on artisanal products that demonstrate time-consuming craftsmanship, such as hand-woven, locally produced textiles.

In collaboration with each artisan, Saran designs and manufactures a modern, uniquely Thai product and markets it through his channels. They split profits evenly. 'I want to dedicate the brand to people who are considered underdogs and feel like they don't belong anywhere,' Saran says, explaining that the brand draws its name from former British prime minister Theresa May's speech at the 2016 Conservative Party conference: 'If you believe you are a citizen of the world, you are a citizen of nowhere.'

Saran had become disillusioned with 56thStudio, where he counted some of Thailand's wealthiest families among his client list. 'I was so eager to do things that were big and epic but, after I'd created a few installations for some high-profile clients, my mood changed,' he says.

One client spent thousands of pounds on an installation, only to destroy it the next day. 'You know you're burning money and you're only creating it to satisfy the urges of the rich,' Saran explains. 'I'm not an anti-capitalist but, as a creative person, there are other things to do to leave your footprints behind.'

Spending time among the local craftspeople, he realized how much more there was to their product stories, noticing the opportunity to strengthen them and make them more 'relevant'.

To help, why not set up a brand that would take traditional Thai crafts and reshape them into contemporary design pieces? Think: the common glass holders found in restaurants, but with fresh-looking graphic patterns – or stools, popular among street-food vendors, recreated in different shapes, patterns and textures.

Citizen of Nowhere's range of products has since ballooned and, with it, the need for a space for its clients to experience it. In 2020, Saran launched Citizen Tea Canteen, a traditional tea room that also stocks Citizen of Nowhere bags, tea containers, teacups and more.

'When you walk into a mall, you only spend like 15 minutes having a look and buying – or not,' Saran says. 'If [there's] something else, like food and drink, you spend more time and the brand philosophy seeps in. I want to communicate that craft can be anything. It could be a T-shirt, [a] glass or the things you eat.'

Saran isn't interested in mass-produced products. Citizen of Nowhere works with a community of local artisans who produce in small amounts and who take great pride in their craft. 'For me, the only sustainable way to develop local craft is to connect the makers with the markets,' he says.

The interior of the store mirrors his vision and is an eclectic mix of thrifted vintage art, fabric samples and secondhand furniture.

'The aesthetic
that I represent is
things that people
consider kitschy.'

Sourcing from Bangkok's abundant shops is a huge part of Saran's day-to-day life. 'A lot of Thai crafts are viewed as old-fashioned. The only way to reinvent the wheel was to start a brand to connect all the dots myself,' he says. 'Otherwise, you end up talking to the same very old grandma and grandpa who've been doing the same things for 40 years – they don't know how to market their products.

'I did some research about the craft situation in Thailand and I found out there are a lot of pain points and obstacles that can be solved with storytelling and design,' says Saran. Through Citizen of Nowhere, Thai craft culture is being introduced to a brand-new audience both around the world and in Thailand.

Thai tea culture is central to the story that Citizen of Nowhere tells and tying it to the handmade crafts allows a new audience to experience it. The drinks list offers a variety of Thai milk teas, all of which come from local farmers, so it's 'linked within the same concept', Saran says.

'There are a lot of pain points and obstacles that can be solved with storytelling and design.'

MØRNING.FYI AND FERAL

Two creative agencies embracing slow living — and a rewilding project.

For more than a decade, Lydia Pang and her husband, Roo Williams, jumped between various jobs in London and across the US, including, for Lydia, a stint as global design director at Nike. In 2020, they returned to a remote part of Wales, where they first met as teenagers, and moved into an old stone house in the tiny village of Llanarth.

Here, they each launched their own creative agency and, equally as important, settled into a much slower lifestyle and a rewilding project. To call it a pace change would be a huge understatement, but it's exactly what they wanted.

'We never really decided to be here,' says Lydia of moving back to Wales. 'We just decided never to leave.'

After studying history of art at The Courtauld Institute of Art, Lydia eventually became the head of visual content at M&C Saatchi, a global advertising agency. In 2015, she and Roo moved to New York, where they both landed jobs at Anomaly, a digital advertising agency. They found life there fun but intense, and it encouraged them to start looking for a deeper connection to nature, as well as themselves.

'New York's a beautiful but transient city,' Lydia reflects. 'There's a competitive energy and you can't help but be sucked into it. I didn't like that version of myself.'

With its outdoors culture, Portland, Oregon, where Lydia moved to work for Nike in 2020, felt like a logical move. But the outbreak of Covid-19 limited their opportunities to explore. When they returned to Wales for Christmas, they realized it was just the place they needed to be – so, they both quit their jobs and committed to putting down roots in the countryside.

Alongside Sam Jackson, who she worked with at Nike, Lydia set up MØRNING.FYI, a creative strategy studio. Meanwhile, Roo, a developer who previously worked at Twitter, launched Feral, a product and service design studio that aims to increase the wellbeing of people and the planet.

Pointing to an example of a recent project, Roo says: 'We're working with one of Wales' most economically deprived schools to create an outdoor program, where children will learn about the relationships between living things through creating a regenerative garden and growing their own food.' Alongside this work, Feral is also building a digital platform that enables local communities to come together and create gardens using regenerative principles.

Today, MØRNING.FYI has 30 staff, most of whom work from a London office. Lydia visits once a month but, otherwise, she runs the agency from the Welsh woodland. Initially, she felt like she was missing out and adding less value, but she's come to learn that distance and objectivity have their benefits.

She and Roo have also recently moved into a new home, which is much warmer and spacious, with several outhouses that they're going to convert into cooking areas. 'There are little woods that surround us,' Lydia says. 'We wanted to feel submerged in the trees.'

Setting up their own studios has allowed Lydia and Roo to work on their own terms, with slow mornings, which they spend walking with Betty, their miniature pinscher dog, or hiking in the afternoons.

'Designing the business – the benefits, the four-day work week, the operating model – in service of creativity and boundaries has been really satisfying,' says Lydia.

'We talk a lot about rewilding of the consciousness.'

Transitioning to this slower pace of life brought its own struggles. Lydia, who'd become accustomed to what she calls the 'toxic, girl-boss productivity energy' of New York, feared her work would suffer. 'I almost had to decode,' she says.

It became easier when Lydia and Roo moved into a 16th-century cottage near the field where they married. The place needed renovating – the previous tenant had lived there for 50 years – but it soon felt like their own. The couple started growing fruits and vegetables and Roo began rewilding a nearby meadowland for biodiversity.

'I think we needed to do it, to bed in,' Roo says. Soon, they were feeling more creative than ever, he adds, 'because we had this perspective.'

'We talk a lot about rewilding land, and that's of great interest, but we also talk a lot about rewilding of the consciousness,' Lydia says. 'Untaming all of these things that have pushed us away from each other, from our connection to nature.'

TRAVEL AND THE GREAT OUTDOORS

A more global and diverse community
is shaping today's travel industry. Here are
some areas of opportunities to look out for.

Emma Mulholland
on Holiday makes
unisex graphic T-shirts
(above) with slogans that
encapsulate the carefree
feeling of a vacation.

The travel industry has had a rough couple of years (who doesn't remember the pandemic?). But now, the concept of travel is bringing new brands to life and, with fewer gatekeepers, the market for everything from sunscreen to suitcases is up for grabs.

$$\boxed{\text{PART ONE}}$$

Niche necessities

It seems like a much more diverse and exciting era for travel has finally arrived. At last, the industry has adapted to consider new ways of living and working, and there's plenty of inspiration for businesses that want to align themselves with the future of travel. And, although old-school products used to dominate the market for travel essentials and experiences, there's never been a better time than now to launch your dream travel business.

Vacation, co-founded by Marty Bell in 2020, sells a range of products that include sunscreen, after-sun gels, face mists and SPF lip balms. Its packaging and marketing have an aesthetic that screams eighties resort. Now seen by many as an essential for a trip to the beach or a weekend getaway, the brand has aligned itself with the mood of what it means to be on vacation.

Connecting to the same idea, designer Emma Mulholland makes what she describes as 'your ultimate holiday wardrobe' with her brand, Emma Mulholland on Holiday. Her colorful, patterned sundresses, swimsuits and linen trousers can all easily squeeze into a suitcase, along with matching towels, tote bags, beach pouches and pool robes.

'I want people to bring the idea of what they feel like on holiday home with them,' says Emma. She pivoted from running her eponymous high-fashion couture brand to a more casual, travel-focused one in 2017. 'My new collection includes sweaters with "Someone on holiday loves me" [printed on them] so, even if you're not away, you can still feel it.'

The amount of money that people spend on an individual trip tends to increase every year and, with the influence of TikTok vacation wardrobe hauls and destination inspiration videos, the desire to travel (or to feel like you are) is stronger than ever. The rise of TikTok as a marketing tool for travel brands is huge, with nearly 80% of people on the platform choosing where they travel or what they purchase for a trip because of content they've seen on the app.

But Melbourne-based travel accessories brand July wants longevity to be the key to its business, not just something for a single trip. Its personalizable suitcases, travel tote bags and luggage tags were developed after its co-founders, Athan Didaskalou and Richard Li, read more than 4,000 reviews of similar items and worked out the pain points for customers. After the pandemic, with the total closure of Australia's borders, the business nearly collapsed, with a 95% loss of revenue. But, now that overseas travel is an option again, July has recovered, made itself a go-to brand for travelers and launched in the US and the UK.

Businesses are rebranding beach umbrellas, pool inflatables, drink coolers, towels, sunhats and skin tints that make you look sun-kissed as essential travel items. Plus, they're exploring the idea of what a travel brand can be for the younger generation. And, if there's something that everyone agrees on, it's that we all feel our best on vacation – and brands are getting smarter at tapping into this feeling.

'I want people to bring the idea of what they feel like on holiday home with them.'

(PART TWO)

The great outdoors

'We're here to better represent ourselves, people of color and, specifically, black people in the outdoor space.'

The outdoors is for everyone, yet the products that facilitate its exploration often seem limited to a select few. For the past 20 or so years, traditional legacy brands like Patagonia, The North Face and Columbia have dominated the sector, in terms of revenue as well as aesthetic and attitudes. New brands are making significant efforts to diversify and include new communities in travel and outdoors-focused experiences like hiking, mountain climbing and biking. This explosion of brands in the outdoors space has completely changed the way that getting out and exploring nature has been perceived.

For Jahmicah Dawes, being in the outdoors industry isn't just about taking up space, but diversifying it. Growing up in Texas, Jahmicah always loved the outdoors. He originally went to college to pursue dreams of working with horses, but this interest evolved into a deep appreciation for creating and curating functional fashion for other outdoorsy folks. 'When I make something with my hands – oh my gosh,' he says. 'The feeling is better than breathing.'

Jahmicah runs Slim Pickins Outfitters, a retail store specializing in all things outdoors, with his wife Heather. 'We're family-owned and operated in the truest sense of the word – because families, they're the ones that help bind the vision and invested in it with you.' The shop is designed to be as inclusive as possible and a large part of Slim Pickins' ethos is about incorporating the family's identity into the business. 'We're here to better show representation for ourselves, our brand, but also people of color and, specifically, black people in the outdoor space.'

Between fly-fishing, going to the park, doing community yoga and hosting bonfires in his backyard, Jahmicah is always eager to bring people together. 'If you [can] make it, we love to have you. And people show up.' He looks forward to a growing number of black outdoor retailers. 'I know we're not monolithic,' he says. 'We were the first but, now, we're not the only.' He's eager

to continue building these spaces and is confident about what's to come to the outdoors industry.

From female hiking collectives like Hike Clerb to Flock Together, a birdwatching collective for people of color based in London, the scene is becoming more inclusive than it ever has been. Hike Clerb isn't just a walking group – it's also a non-profit that's collaborated with the likes of big sports and outdoors brands like HOKA, Arc'teryx, Nike, Salomon and The North Face, all while 'centering a historically under-represented and marginalized group of people', explains founder Evelynn Escobar.

At Utah's Zion National Park in 2017, Evelynn, then 23, was trekking along jagged trails and looking out upon the spectacular rock formations when she suddenly realized that she hadn't seen another woman for the entire duration of her trip

– only middle-aged white men. 'I knew I couldn't be the only black [or] brown woman interested in this,' says Evelynn, who started hiking as a teenager with her aunt in Los Angeles. 'I knew I had to get more of us out here,' she says.

Joy Howard is the founder of Early Majority, an outerwear brand for women. As a keen hiker, the former vice-president of marketing at Patagonia was frustrated with what she calls the take-down effect – where women's kit would be an inferior rendition of men's garments, lacking in technical ability and design – and decided to create a brand to rectify this.

Since its launch in 2021, Early Majority has partnered with female-led collectives including Athene Club, GorpGirls and Feminist Bird Club. Joy thinks that the outdoor industry is changing as 'women are starting their own brands' and servicing this need. It's clear that the old guard of heritage brands no longer holds the same space as they once did and that the face of the outdoors is changing. Now's the time to be a part of it.

Evelynn Escobar *(in blue)* aimed her hiking club specifically at women of color and Indigenous people.

The Maçakızı hotel,
which relocated in 2000,
has 53 bedrooms
and 21 suites, all with
king-size beds and
many with breathtaking
views of the sea.

(PART THREE)

Family matters

With many hotels around the world being absorbed into global conglomerates, family-run brands have a strong appeal. The idea that a hotel has been passed down through generations and preserved to retain its original charm and character is key to how many people choose where they stay when they travel.

In the late seventies, Ayla Emiroğlu moved to the city of Bodrum on the coastline of Turkey when it was just a sleepy seaside town. She opened a small hotel with a bar and a restaurant; today, Maçakızı is one of Turkey's most in-demand hotels. 'My mother had a way of looking out for people and making them feel special. That's still how I want every guest to feel when they're here,' says her son, Sahir Erozan, who now runs the hotel following a career mostly spent launching restaurants across the US.

Since Sahir took over operations in 1998, the hotel has grown significantly, with renovations across the property, additions of a private villa for larger parties and even a boat. Even so, the core values remain the same. 'It was all about the food for my mom. She'd have Mick Jagger at her table, but she'd still have just simple Turkish food on the menu. If the ingredients are quality, it's all you need,' he explains.

Sahir says that there are still a handful of guests who remember his mother being behind the bar. 'It's all about returning guests for me. I want us to be part of their life.'

Black-and-white photographs of Sahir's family from the seventies are spread across the common areas of the hotel and feature on the

hotel's website. It's a huge part of the brand narrative and a core reason why guests book (and keep coming back). 'It was never my original plan to run my mother's business – I had an entirely separate life over in America, but who wouldn't want to live here?' says Sahir.

Sometimes a family-run hotel isn't something that's passed down – often, it's a choice to start something new for future generations. The Betsy hotel on Ocean Drive on Miami's South Beach is run by husband and wife Jonathan Plutzik and Lesley Goldwasser. Jonathan left a career in finance to renovate the art-deco hotel and brought it back to its former glory in 2009. He now runs it alongside his wife, sister Deborah, and son Zachary, who's the hotel's managing director. It's family-owned and operated, with

details down to the coasters featuring the handwriting of Jonathan's father, Hyam Plutzik, who was a Pulitzer Prize finalist. The family's golden retriever dogs, Betsy and Rosa, are often seen running through the hallways.

For guests who have the choice of any of the huge chain hotels on one of the most populous strips of accommodation in the world, they choose to return to The Betsy because of the sense of familial comfort.

As people seek more authentic experiences, family-run hotels will continue to be a selling point. When asked if he hopes that any of his children will want to carry on the future of Maçakızı, Sahir laughs. 'They'll have their own lives,' he says, 'but, ultimately, I hope they want to come back – just like I did'.

'My mother had a way of making people feel special. That's how I want every guest to feel when they're here.'

CASA
LAWA

Overlooking Mount Etna, a guesthouse, chef residency and orchard.

The serenity found at Casa Lawa, a guesthouse located in rural Sicily overlooking Mount Etna, bears little resemblance to one of Lukas Lewandowski's previous lives. For five years, Lukas worked as a bouncer. Today, instead of being surrounded by loud music and drunk clubbers, he wakes up each morning to the sound of songbirds in the garden and the smell of fresh cherries.

Founded in 2022, Casa Lawa (meaning 'lava house', in a melding of Italian and Polish) is the work of Lukas and his Dutch husband, Merijn Gillis. It's a place where they combine their passions for food, design and hospitality by hosting guests from all around the world and, together, they take part in workshops on painting, fermenting, baking and more. Sometimes the pair will cook but, more often, they'll host residencies, inviting their favorite chefs and bakers to deliver menus that change with the seasons.

When the weather's good, Lukas and Merijn arrange wild foraging walks, teaching guests to taste plants and pick fruits that they'll turn into jam. Guests also learn to make chestnut honey, which they can enjoy on toast with whipped ricotta, alongside kombucha and juices. On a still night, they can experience the volcano rumbling or even spitting lava.

Lukas spent some of his professional life consulting for brands across fashion, food and design, but he was also deeply connected to cooking. He thought about opening a restaurant, but then the pandemic happened. A new idea emerged: to have a large, open space in the countryside where he and Merijn could host people for days, weeks or longer. All together, they could indulge in the joys of community and delicious food and drink.

So, in the spring of 2021 the couple began house-hunting, starting in northern Italy. They wanted something authentic, 'not something new', Lukas says, and with lots of space where they could 'organize retreats and host dinner parties'. They wanted to grow fruits and vegetables.

What they found in September of that year, in Italy's southernmost region, was Casa Lawa, a 400-meter-square house located between the two municipalities of Milo and Sant'Alfio. Built in 1812 from lava stone, it boasts views of the sea and Mount Etna and has thick walls to keep it cool in summer and warm in the winter. It also has 10 acres of fruit orchards, where they grow cherries, apples and pears for cider. The garden is always buzzing with butterflies and other wildlife and, during the colder months, guests can light a fire in one of the six fireplaces.

'The place checked all the boxes,' Lukas recalls. 'It has a soul. From that point, we didn't want to see anything else.'

Being so old, the house needed renovating – plastering, painting, and a lot of gardening. They filled the property with furniture and, the next summer, began renting out one of the bedrooms; later, a second. A swimming pool is on the way and the outside shed will become another bedroom, which will allow them to host six guests. It's deliberately small and intimate. 'It's first and foremost a place of community,' says Lukas.

'It's a stay for people who like to connect with people,' Lukas explains. 'People who are curious about food, who are curious about design and who are curious about making wine. It's for people who are passionate about life.'

For guests, breakfast is served daily and includes fresh ricotta, avocados from a tree on the property, local seasonal fruit and eggs that are shared at a large communal table.

There are two guestrooms at Casa Lawa – the Sea Room and the Volcano Room *(right)*. The Sea Room features original terracotta tiles and Italian-designed furnishings, while the Volcano Room – the more spacious of the two – has its own personal living room with a Nuvolone sofa, a modular design piece created by Rino Maturi in the seventies. Both rooms have a king-size bed created by sustainability-focused brand COCO-MAT.

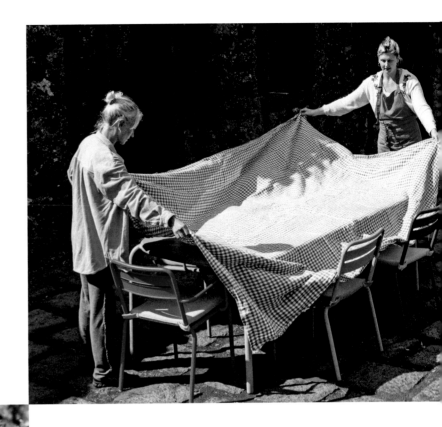

The origins of Casa Lawa can be traced back to Poland, where Lukas was born. He loved fashion but his parents encouraged him to study psychology, which compounded his feeling of being out of place. 'Being a homosexual in Poland is a bit of a thing – I always felt like an outsider,' he says. 'At some point, I just wanted to try living abroad.'

In 2012, he moved to Berlin, where he would buy and sell vintage clothes and work at a popular nightclub. One day, he met Merijn and

together they moved to Amsterdam, where they'd host large dinner parties.

'Looking back, I think it was a way of digging for a community – a sense of belonging,' says Lukas. 'I had a difficult childhood, so I think I try to compensate for that by being with my friends and creating a modern family.'

They sold their home in Amsterdam (though they've kept a small apartment) and moved into Casa Lawa in November 2021.

'I think it was a way of digging for a community – a sense of belonging.'

'The place checked all
the boxes. It has a soul.'

WANG & SÖDERSTRÖM

A design studio melding the digital and physical worlds.

Anny Wang and Tim Söderström, the Copenhagen-based duo behind art and design studio Wang & Söderström, may be best known for their digital creations, but they're not fans of the stripped-down, white-space-filled default that makes up most digital environments these days.

'It's almost like the typical image of heaven that people have – very bright, only clouds, as if that would be the perfect place,' Tim explains. 'I'm not so sure at all. We think digital shouldn't be used to create utopias of how great and minimalistic life could be. Humans are messy and we want to create spaces for them to *feel* human in.'

Wang & Söderström's digital creations appear online and across social media, as well as in person at museums and galleries from London to Tokyo, Paris to Miami. Plus, the studio has collaborated with some of the world's leading creative brands, such as Burberry, Nike, The New York Times and the Nobel Prize Organization. For a campaign with luggage brand RIMOWA, it surrounded a baby-pink suitcase with large floating globules. For lifestyle and furniture brand HAY, it created a collection of physical objects inspired by its digital motifs.

Anny and Tim met in Copenhagen in 2011, having both moved from Sweden because Denmark's institutions place architecture and design in the art faculty, whereas Sweden lumps them into the technical department. The pair started working together almost as soon as they met, encouraging each other's projects after realizing that they shared an equally ambitious approach to digital design. They became a couple in 2012 and worked for the same architecture firm.

For a few years, their days were made up of double shifts between their nine-to-five jobs and their independent work – until, in 2016, after landing some bigger private projects, the pair rented a space and broke out on their own. Having to suddenly cover bills was scary, Tim says, but it also 'helped to have to pay for the space each month. It made our train have to roll. Plus, we'd been students so recently, we were still very skilled at keeping costs low.'

Today, the two divide their time between client and personal projects, while also working with students at design schools in Copenhagen and Germany. They say that this mentorship is more selfish than selfless, as being around the new generation keeps them on their toes.

Some hard-won government grants have also allowed them to be picky about which brands they agree to work with. 'A good challenge is one where we work both spatially and digitally, and are in charge of a holistic view of the whole project,' explains Anny. 'But we also like working with really big brands as a way of taking a seat at the table, influencing how an ad can look and also carrying our aesthetics into a new realm.'

'We see digital technology as an extension of our real world, not a replacement,' Tim explains. 'We want to use it to push our senses and the way we look at materials in our real life. We're not trying to make a perfect world that doesn't really exist.'

Anny and Tim both used to work until the small hours, but having a child has helped them to switch off a little. But it's also added a moral urgency to their work, because it's heightened their concern that today's children aren't spending time with as many textures as they themselves did in their youth.

'The reason that our images feel tactile and you want to touch them is probably because you have lots of previous experience of how things feel – from sandy to slimy – and grew up touching a lot of things like we did,' Anny explains. 'But, with touchscreens and keyboards, we're evolving to a less and less tactile life.

'Technology today is quite hard, efficiency-driven and commercial, and that takes us away from our senses. Taking a soft approach to digital is also key for us, to make sure we convey our softer values.'

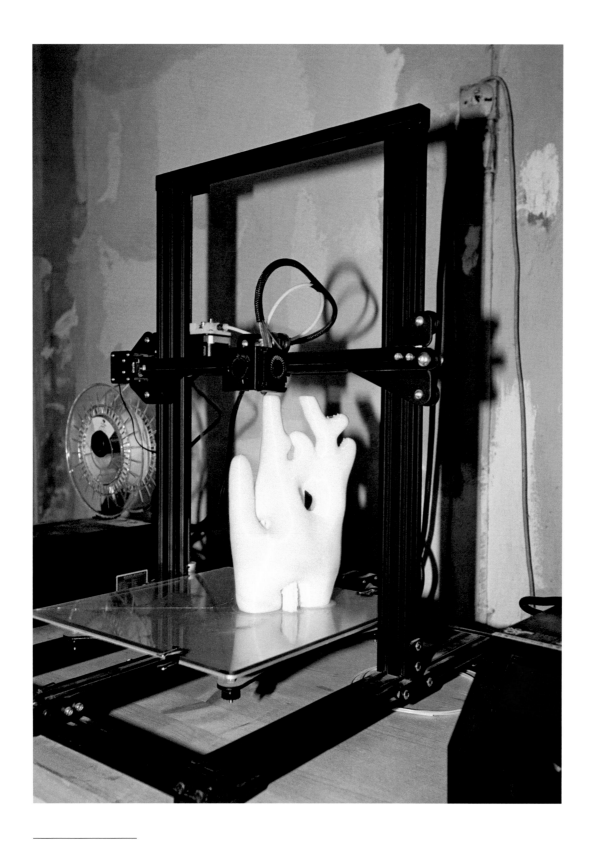

'The space is very much a reflection of how we want our work to be in our reality,' says Tim of their studio workshop. 'It should be in this rough, unpolished world filled with dust and fingerprints but also, at the same time, we have computers that are quite sensitive, so we have space for that. We're molding and messy in one room, and at our computers in the other.'

The duo say that their aversion to digital minimalism comes from a nostalgia for the mess they grew up around in their respective childhood homes. Both of their parents liked to hoard – Tim grew up surrounded by paper bags, screws and lamps, while Anny's home was filled with 'very kitsch Chinese decor, plastic fruits, crafts, plus junky technology everywhere and TVs in every room'.

'We've always been fascinated by one phenomenon: that a lot of materials in the real world are actually quite translucent,' says Anny. 'Take our skin — when you put it up against the sun, it's very translucent.

'Every material is reflecting something without our thinking about it, even stone,' says Tim. 'We like to highlight aspects like that in our designs.'

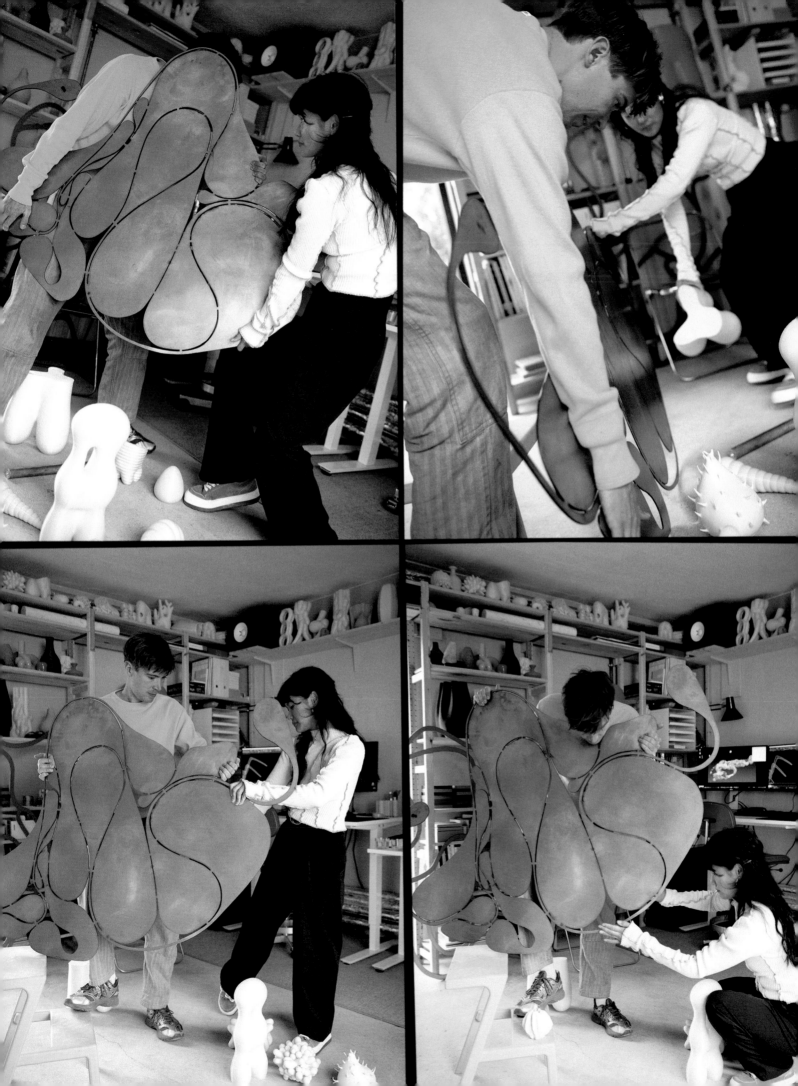

'Humans are messy and we want to create spaces for them to feel human in.'

Anny and Tim emphasize that they don't want to pick up a new tool just for the sake of it, but rather discover where it could fit into their universe. Take 3D printing, for example – while the technology has been around for some time, it's often used for architectural or industrial purposes. Anny and Tim used the tech to turn their hyper-real 3D renderings of textured shapes into tangible objects for their 2017 exhibition Transitional Speculation, blurring the line between physical and digital.

TREVAREF ABRIKKEN

A hotel and restaurant between a fjord and the mountains.

Trevarefabrikken, a hotel, restaurant, bar and cultural space, sits on the islands of Henningsvær, Norway, overlooking the sea. Its founders, two pairs of brothers – Martin Hjelle, Andreas Hjelle, Mats Alfsen and Andreas Alfsen – never intended to start the project. Hailing from Bergen, they'd set off on a hiking trip to central Norway in the summer of 2014. The weather turned sour, but they saw that it was beautiful in the Lofoten archipelago.

After some miscalculations, they ended up in the fishing village of Henningsvær – 20km from Svolvær, Lofoten's unofficial capital – with 30°C weather. They slept on the bare grass, hiking by day and soaking up the sun by night. One day, they visited a bar and had drinks with a singer. They took him on a hike to see the midnight sun and he told them about Trevarefabrikken, an abandoned multi-purpose factory. So, they headed off to take a look.

Built in the forties, over time Trevarefabrikken had served as a place to do shrimping, whale canning, cod-liver-oil steaming and woodworking (which the factory is named after). 'In the steam room, you opened the service doors and this breathtaking view of the sun, mountains and sea came flooding in,' says Martin. The two pairs of brothers suddenly felt possessive. 'My brother said: "We can't let anyone else buy this,"' Martin explains. They'd felt welcomed by the local community and wanted to stick around.

With no support from the bank, the four pooled their savings to buy the building for around 2 million kr ($190,000). They planned to renovate it alongside their regular work and, over the next few summers, they invited friends to live in the building while they helped out.

In the summer of 2016, they fixed the roof, which was showing signs of erosion. They managed to get funding due to the building's cultural heritage protection – the roof was built using a special technique of filling up wooden casts with concrete, which wasn't common in a small fishing town like Henningsvær back in the forties. '[The building is] unique from an industrial and architectural point of view. A lot of people came to the factory just to look at the view,' says Martin.

The vision for Trevarefabrikken solidified once they had a bit more money to play with. They opened a small outside bar in 2016, the success of which prompted the bank to approve their loan application. Work on Hermetikken, a bar and restaurant named after its former use as a shrimp cannery, began in 2017, quickly followed by a cafe. The co-founders put on their own music festival, with tickets selling out in under 15 minutes – and the festival continues to this day. Then, in 2018, they built four hotel rooms, with eight more, designed by Jonathan Tuckey Design, following in 2020.

That original gut feeling has taken the founders pretty far. 'A key factor to our success is that we've got a lot of support from the local community,' says Martin. 'People tend to come outside of the main season for Northern Lights hiking and skiing. I think some of the popularity of Henningsvær is due to us.'

Without insulation, the hotel originally couldn't stay open through the winter. The pandemic delayed plans, so 2022 was the first year it could safely stay open for some of the winter. Now, the hotel can accommodate winter skiing trips alongside its summer offerings.

Although the pandemic was a huge blow for the hotel, the founders used the time to get on with renovations. In autumn 2020, they drilled 300-meter-deep wells for a heating pump system that would be powered by geothermal energy.

There are four restaurants on site – a cafe, a pizzeria, a wine bar and a bar-restaurant. The menus are seasonal and make use of Norwegian ingredients – a sweet mushroom pizza features Aalan Gård goat's cheese, while the bar serves several Norwegian ciders.

'We had to go back
to our studies and
regular jobs, but
we couldn't say no.'

The four co-founders
were tipped off about
the Trevarefabrikken
building by a local they
met in Henningsvær.

'He made us promise
to go look at it,' says Martin.
'We were high off a week
of midnight sun and alcohol.
We had to go back to our
studies and regular jobs,
but we couldn't say no.'

They slept on top of the
mountain and, the next
day, the owner gave them
a tour. 'It was quite run
down,' he says, but its

concrete structure was solid,
with 2,000 square meters
spanning three floors.

Martin says that all four
of them were blown away
by the scenery and nature.
'It's the only place – except
for the school – with a
view towards the ocean,
the Vestfjorden [fjord] and
the mountains,' he says.

Work began on the
building in 2015, with the
help of many volunteers,
who came together for
parties and dinners around
a long table most days.

MIRAI

A bonsai workshop, nursery, creative studio and school.

It takes a certain kind of person – one with tenacity, patience and a serious work ethic – to dedicate themself to learning a craft for six years in a country where they can't even speak the language. Yet that's exactly what Colorado native Ryan Neil did when, shortly after finishing college, he flew to Japan to immerse himself in the art of bonsai.

It's been around 15 years since Ryan returned to the US. In that time, he founded a nursery, creative studio and school called Mirai, which employs a handful of people and is based just outside of Portland in St Helens, Oregon, at the end of a rambling driveway near mountains and forest. There are rows and rows of beautiful bonsai crafted from US natives – conifers, junipers and pines.

'I was the sort of kid who knew at 12 that I wanted to work with bonsai,' Ryan says from the garden. The early introduction to bonsai came by way of The Karate Kid films, where a central character, Mr Miyagi, calmly tends to a number of miniature trees. Following the films, Ryan sought out everything bonsai. 'Once I saw those trees, I thought: this is it.'

When Ryan established Mirai in 2010, he wanted to respect tradition but attract a new generation. He started offering tutelage, attracting apprentices from far-flung places like Australia, France and Slovenia, as well as a steady stream from across the US. In 2017, he pared back his in-person classes and started offering online lessons and educational resources through an in-house production company. 'That's changed the game, as so many people are accessing the information. They're aged 18 to 28 – a very different audience than if you went to a bonsai fair.'

Ryan dedicated himself to learning the traditional art, which dates back to around 600 AD. Halfway through a horticulture degree, he traveled to Japan, where he met Masahiko Kimura, the man known as the father of modern bonsai. 'To my eyes, there was no greater. I told him that I wanted to apprentice and he laughed,' Ryan recalls. After returning to the US, Ryan wrote 22 letters asking for an apprenticeship; by the 23rd, Masahiko granted him one.

Ryan spent six years in Japan's Saitama Prefecture, where he was the first western person to complete an apprenticeship under Masahiko – an experience that was as grueling as it was rewarding.

'There was never any praise,' Ryan recalls. It was a difficult time for him. 'I just went inwards and handled it that way.'

Despite the difficulties, Ryan is grateful for his time with Masahiko. 'I wouldn't change a thing about my journey,' he says emphatically. 'It took a master like him to bring out that self-understanding, that self-belief and the confidence that it takes to do what I'm doing now,' Ryan says. 'Of course, that doesn't mean you don't get some scars and scrapes along the way. That pathway wouldn't be for everyone.'

'I want this place to be somewhere that keeps making bonsai ninjas that can do bad-ass shit – people who blend science and art form. I want to see bonsai at MoMA in New York, at the Guggenheim. I believe it'll get there at some point.'

Mirai is open by appointment only, and its address is undisclosed. A steady crop of bonsai enthusiasts and students from around the world flock to Oregon to learn about the art.

'Outside of Japan, bonsai is really on the decline,' explains Ryan. 'It's dying because it hasn't kept pace with the modernizing world and the mentality of younger people who are needed to carry the torch forward.'

Mirai's name was inspired by the Japanese word for 'future', and a huge part of Ryan's passion is to protect the skills and teach them to the next generation. 'It refers not to the immediate future, but to a distant dream – a romantic thought, the future yet to come, ever out of reach, unobtainable and always evolving,' he says.

'These tiny trees are such a microcosm of what can exist in the relationship between humans and the wild – of human stewardship of the natural world,' explains Ryan. 'I think for many in today's world, it also answers that "call to the wild" – but in a way that you don't have to be so [distant] from the urban.'

'I have several students [who] are professionals now [and] are quite successful – that's based on their own ambitions and a little bit of the knowledge that we [gave] them,' says Ryan.

'I hope they go off and do their own thing and we continue to expand the community. They have their outreach and their touch points and we [can] grow this population that's practicing at a higher level,' he says. The classes are a crucial element of Mirai and make the business sustainable. 'I need to teach people to continue to have a student core that finds value in what we do,' he says.

'I need to teach people to continue to have a core that finds value in what we do.'

CREATIVE INDUSTRIES

Social media has put rocket fuel into art, design
and fashion – making launching your own business
in these areas more accessible than ever before.

PART ONE

Time to get creative

There's never been a better time to launch a dream business in the creative industries. Just ask Peder Cho, a former accountant whose passion for upcycling old NBA jerseys led him to document his creative process on TikTok. Now his brand Utopia shows on international runways, with Peder creating custom pieces for brands such as Skims, Nike and KidSuper.

There's also Kelsey Floyd. From her home in Tampa, Florida, she tried throwing pottery for the first time in 2020 and, just two years later, is making a living full-time from her mixed media ceramics and has exhibited at Paris Design Week.

And look at Montreal-based artist Gab Bois, whose career blew up when she moved from Tumblr to Instagram to share her surreal images of, say, beanie hats filled with fruit loop cereal and oyster-shell smartphones. She, too, has an impressive list of commissions, with the likes of Glossier, Marc Jacobs and Mercedes-Benz.

Canadian artist Gab Bois creates surprising, sometimes unsettling works that use food purely for its aesthetic value.

FIND YOUR NICHE

These three creatives are symbolic of the new wave of individuals and small business owners exploring creative and artistic pursuits, and building thriving new careers from them.

Since 2020, more than 165 million creators joined the global creator economy. At least in part, the boom may have been prompted by lockdowns around the globe. But, if this was the spark, then platforms like Instagram, TikTok and Substack have kept the fire burning, helping creators experiment in exciting new ways. Around one in four people are now creators, contributing their work to online spaces.

Not long ago, a career in the creative industries meant years of study, paid for through a tapestry of unrelated casual jobs and then plenty more years earning just enough to fund the work itself. And while making it big and keeping afloat remain serious challenges for any creative, social media has afforded greater access to the sector. The quality of a creator's work and their unique voice carries far more weight than the number of art dealers they know or which degree programs they've completed.

'Creators are no longer beholden to cultural gatekeepers or arbiters of what's good and what's not,' says Dan Weinstein, co-founder of Underscore Talent, which helps creators, artists and business owners manage all aspects of their careers, from consumer products to brand deals and content distribution. 'It's much easier to create your own niche or find the one that needs you, paving the way to build a business and monetize it in a ton of different ways.'

'It's much easier to create your own niche or find the one that needs you.'

CREATIVE COMMERCE

Social search is on the rise – nearly 40% of young adults prefer using TikTok and Instagram for internet searches over Google – and it aligns particularly well with the creative arts. Shoppers can identify new, independent brands at speed, creating a personalized collection of items to buy. Platforms like TikTok Shop have smoothed the path to purchase, but endless hashtags and the hard sell aren't commonplace for this cohort of creators. Instead, they use platforms to reveal their process through inspiring and informative content like how-tos or time-lapse videos.

One huge shift is the opportunity to build personality around creative commerce. As Dan points out: 'It used to be that if you were selling a piece of art or a rug, a consumer had to really want that item.' With personality built around the physical product, 'people are more receptive to buying it because they like you', he says.

Exposure to other people's work and creative journeys can prompt the adoption of new techniques, with all kinds of content illuminating pathways people might never have considered. Plus, it boosts freedom and flexibility – trying something out feels less risky when you can gauge real-time feedback. Now more than ever, creators are throwing things at the wall and seeing what sticks. With an expansive toolbox of spaces and mediums to communicate an artistic journey and its outcomes, creative industries really are yours for the taking.

(PART TWO)

Opportunities in design

Before social media dominated, interior design was veiled in exclusivity. Buying required heavy research and time spent collating brands, if not the expertise of an interior designer. Now design fans are consulting trends on TikTok, curating dream-bedroom mood boards on Pinterest and messaging furniture sellers on Instagram. And that's all before actually making a purchase.

As lockdowns prompted an epic homemaking drive, interiors searches and purchasing through social media platforms exploded. According to research firm Technavio, the market for online home decor is expected to increase by nearly $60 billion from 2021 to 2026, with around 9% growth every year.

The viral potential of design pieces is a major shift and, when it happens, creators have to be ready to scale fast. Multidisciplinary artist Sean Brown launched his homeware line with rugs in the shape of nineties vinyls. In 2020, his first tweet about them went viral and Curves, which Sean founded with business partner Iva Golubovic, snowballed from there. It's now stocked in stores around the world, including Canadian retailer SSENSE and Kith stores in Paris, Miami, New York and Tokyo. A collection of inflatable furniture was another viral win.

A LICENSE TO KILN

One particular design discipline has been transformed by social media. Open TikTok or Instagram and ceramicists are seemingly everywhere. There's an intimacy emerging between makers and shoppers, too. New Yorker Laura Chautin intersperses product shots with photos of her dog and partner on Instagram, while Jessica Gregson of Luxe Home Decor uses TikTok to share the pitfalls associated with making her clay-resin pieces.

Accounts collating and spotlighting independent ceramicists, such as *@potteryforall* and *@pottery_videos*, help spread reach even

Ego *(above)* is a collection from Curves by Sean Brown, which nods to Vietnamese designer Quasar Khanh, a pioneer of inflatable furniture in the sixties.

Miista *(below)* is a shoe brand with a focus on environmental and social sustainability.

further, with ASMR-style videos of ceramicists at the wheel especially popular – check out the TikTok hashtag #OddlySatisfyingPottery. There's an appetite for weird and unsettling one-of-a-kinds – for example, Alma Berrow's clay ashtrays stuffed with the debris of daily life (which she likens to portraits) and Katy Stubbs' modern-day tragedies on her giant pots.

LIKE, SHARE, SUBSCRIBE

The endless amount of user-generated content means that simply typing in a trend or style on a social media platform unlocks thousands of posts, showing how people have styled something in their own homes. Nick Dynan has been working as a graphic designer in London for more than a decade, but learned pottery through YouTube tutorials – he now creates swear jars and vases for his side hustle, Me Old China. His In the Wild Instagram Stories Highlight reveals his excitement when he sees one of his creations in a real-life living room or on a kitchen table. That's the kind of thrill that, no matter how big your audience, hopefully never disappears.

'It used to be that if you were selling a piece of art, a consumer had to want that item. Now people are more receptive to buying it because they like you.'

PART THREE

Opportunities in fashion

The role of social media to market and sell clothes is changing. In some corners of the industry, social media breaks down barriers; in others, it's being leveraged by those who prioritize cultural capital over high follower counts.

British streetwear brand Corteiz launched in 2017 with a community-driven approach to fashion, announcing releases via a private Instagram account and a password-protected website. And it seems to be working: in the space of six years, Corteiz has already reached cult status and exploded in popularity, kicking off 2023 with its first major label co-sign with Nike.

IF YOU KNOW, YOU KNOW

Many other brands are also employing similar tactics. Streetwear label Bene Culture's drops have secret passwords, while its Insta posts are a warm and inviting mix of stylized short films, clips of T-shirts being printed and Instax shots of its store in Birmingham, UK.

'Social media can be an amplifier and a tool, but it's not a magic bullet,' says Dan from Underscore Talent. 'It doesn't allow you to make a subpar product or ignore the fundamentals of building a business.' If you're building something, he continues, 'it needs to start with: what's the product? Is it great and do people want it?'

Particularly among sustainable brands and designers using waste textiles, becoming known for one specific garment and engaging with a dedicated but small audience who'll buy multiple versions of the item can safeguard longevity. Tom Robinson runs Thheme from a warehouse in Vancouver, making hats from upcycled materials that he sources with his partner Jamie Dawes, who's at the helm of womenswear label Fyoocher. Sometimes the couple even create items from the same deadstock fabric.

To give a glimpse into the execution of an idea, content can be pared back and perhaps a little shaggy around the edges. Pulling back the curtain is a smart tactic for solo designers and bigger independents alike – Galicia-born Laura Villasenin's footwear brand Miista often posts videos of its leather-makers at their sewing machines. In an industry that's often criticized for sustainability issues and a lack of supply-chain transparency, letting the cameras inside the warehouse can't be a bad thing.

BE THE EXPERT

Acting as the eyes and ears for tastemakers is becoming an industry in itself. Menswear-adjacent Substack publication Blackbird Spyplane – created by Jonah Weiner, a culture journalist, and Apple talent scout Erin Wylie – delivers twice-weekly drops into thousands of inboxes around the world. Billed as 'your number-one source for style, culture and unbeatable recon', it has a scrappy, zine-like feel that stands apart from other fashion media brands.

Proving the sky's the limit with a digital publication, Lawrence Schlossman and James Harris, the duo behind hit fashion and lifestyle podcast Throwing Fits, have moved from commentating into curating, designing capsule collections with British menswear brand Percival and online retailer MR PORTER.

179

(PART FOUR)

Opportunities in art

Jaime Levin had always wanted to build a business around postcards. He picked up a fondness for them on his trips around the world. Originally from Melbourne, in 2019, he moved from Denmark to Oaxaca, Mexico, to find a job at an architecture firm and perfect his Spanish, but he fell in love with the city and, alongside work at coffee shops, started drawing local businesses.

'It clicked that I could create a more local version of a postcard, so people could get a memory of a cafe, restaurant or even piece of ceramics they'd experienced here,' he says.

Word of the project, which he named Once In Oaxaca, spread fast on Instagram and it wasn't long before businesses and individuals were approaching him for commissions – whether it was the local dentist or someone wanting to keep the memory of their grandma's house alive. Jaime credits the project for helping to build his community and integrate him into the city.

After four years in Oaxaca, he's making a living from his postcards and has opened a workshop and gallery space in Jalatlaco, an artistic neighborhood of the city. 'I've never worked in art or really created it before, so I'm just rolling with how Once In Oaxaca will evolve going forward,' he says.

WATCH AND LEARN

The ability to document a project through social media is one reason why artists are finding success on these platforms. Jaime says that with a lot of people he follows, he's interested in their creative journey – sometimes more so than the products they make. With creative mediums often existing in totally different silos, social media platforms offer a few central spaces to coalesce, which is useful when trying out a new discipline. With many new-generation creators being self-taught, they aren't beholden to staying in their lane. The average creator is involved in 2.8 artistic pursuits, according to a report by software company Adobe, and social media allows people to embrace these multiplicities all at once.

Aspiring creators who perhaps haven't explored their creative sides look to visual platforms for education. Toronto-based graphic designer Ben Courtice, founder of creative studio Boring Friends, shares trend round-ups and design processes through his TikTok account. Painter Anna Topuriya enjoys how Holistic Correspondence, her publication on newsletter platform Substack, lets her share her work on her own terms, without the pressures of social media. It's a blank canvas that centralizes engagement with a community. Some artists use the platform to sell courses, explore creative methods or spread the word about upcoming exhibitions.

ALWAYS HAVE FUN

Inspired by the principles of *ikebana*, an ancient Japanese approach to flower arranging, Frukebana came about during the pandemic. Floral stylist Kasia Borowiecka and photographer Olivia Bennett ran virtual workshops inviting attendees to gather vegetables, fruits and flowers to draw, then create and photograph sculptures from them, ikebana-style.

As well as building a body of their own Frukebana designs, the pair now run small in-person sessions and have been invited to design concepts for various brands. 'Frukebana is linked with my day-to-day job, but it's reminded me to have fun and not be afraid to experiment more, as some of these ideas do convert into paid opportunities,' says Kasia, who runs a floral design studio in London called Cosmos&Plums.

Jaime believes that one of the biggest challenges in the creative industry is connecting an idea to making a living. 'Trust yourself and go where the project takes you,' he says. 'I'm someone who has to resolve everything in my mind before taking action, but Once In Oaxaca has opened my eyes to the possibilities when I take risks.'

'I used to joke when I started the project: wouldn't it be funny if one day my currency of living is postcards?' he says. 'And it is now, which is just insane.'

Frukebana *(left)* exists at the intersection of many different art forms – ikebana, sculpture, food styling, photography and still-life drawing – giving workshop participants a chance to discover a range of new creative outlets.

In his studio in Oaxaca *(right)*, Jaime Levin is now experimenting with his own ceramics and furniture and, coming full circle, has an architecture project in the works.

'It's reminded me to have fun and not be afraid to experiment more.'

SUNNE VOYAGE

A boat cruise brand that gives back to the local community.

Traveling between Thailand's mainland and its many islands, Winchana Prucksananont Gun Suwannasit always wondered why there weren't any nicer-looking boats that would make the experience of cruising more enjoyable – something different and more luxurious from all the brightly colored boats that seemed to be everywhere.

He also wanted to start his own lucrative business – one that could support the local community and boost tourism in Klaeng district, which is on the coastline of Rayong province in eastern Thailand. Although the area is just a 2.5-hour drive from Bangkok, it's far less popular with tourists than many other similar coastal spots further south.

So, along with four other co-founders – Kittitat Sudprasert, Nittaya Chananukul, Gun Suwannasith and Dhun Packpongphanchai – Winchana (known as Win) set up Sunne Voyage. To get the business started, he found an old, traditional fishing boat and set about transforming it into the company's first vessel, the Voyager. Because he liked the existing natural wooden structure and the detailed jointing, he decided that it was important to not mess around with those key features.

Lots of decorative touches set Sunne Voyage's boats apart. The Voyager's curtains blowing in the wind, Win says, tend to be his customers' favorite. A month-long collaboration in 2022 with design house Marimekko saw the plain white curtains replaced with some of Finnish brand's iconic colorful patterns.

The Voyager also has two stairways leading to the top deck for people to chill, sunbathe or watch the sunset.

On each trip, the boat can visit three islands: Koh Man Nai, Koh Man Klang and Koh Munnork. A full-day trip leaves at 10am, while a half-day trip departs at 1pm. All trips include welcome drinks, infused water, towels, music and the use of an outdoor shower. Guests can enjoy lunch, which will likely feature seasonal fruit and seafood skewers, and activities such as paddle boarding and fishing. Trips don't operate during the rainy season, which is from the end of May to the end of October.

When asked what's special about Sunne Voyage, Win said that it's mainly about the opportunity that it provides to support the lives of local people – creating jobs and allowing them to earn an income from their skills, taking pride in their work and being able to give back to others in the local community.

Another benefit of Sunne Voyage is its potential to teach people about the importance of maintaining the natural environment. Although many local people make a living from the sea, there's a lack of education around the environment and how to best take care of it. Many ditch their cigarettes anywhere they find convenient, Win explains. But, since working with Sunne Voyage, many have come to understand how and why they need to keep the ocean and beach clean. He hopes that his business can continue to help 'make [people] realize that they need to take care of nature and the sea, where they spend their whole lives'.

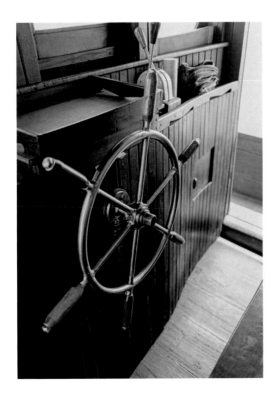

Getting his vision across to the boat builders was one of the most difficult parts of getting Sunne Voyage up and running, according to Win. At first, they didn't really understand how the boat would function. A boat of this size would usually fit about 30 to 40 people in it, but Win wanted it to accommodate only 10 people. Persistence was key.

On each trip, there are one or two members of staff, depending on the size of the group, who'll take care of the customers – everything from welcoming them and guiding them through snorkeling to taking care of the bar and serving food and drinks.

'What's most important for the service on the boat is to give customers some space. Customers want to be taken care of, but they should be feeling comfortable being themselves and able to fully relax here,' says Win. 'The staff have to be ready to [serve] customers [but], at the same time, always keep in mind the customers' privacy.'

'What's most important for the service on the boat is to give customers some space.'

Win's vision goes far beyond the cruising experience. He wants Sunne Voyage to evolve into a brand that shares the unique identities of the different communities and districts of Thailand. He wants to bring out the charm and present the rich culture of each place, whether that be through food, crafts or design, and work with the community, connect people and create products, services and experiences that'll add value to the community and boost the local economy.

'When there's no support from the government,' he says, 'each community has to keep on trying to create new products with their own hands.'

'Each community has to keep on trying to create new products with their own hands.'

'They need to take care of nature and the sea, where they spend their whole lives.'

Combining the craftsmanship of local boat builders with Win's design sensibilities, the boats were transformed to become as you see them today. With their hand-carved, curvy wood and a traditional aesthetic, they're proving hugely popular with tourists and locals alike.

COYOL

A farm-to-table restaurant off the beaten track.

Just outside of the village of Nosara on the Nicoya Peninsula of Costa Rica, at the top of a very steep, winding and dusty road, you'll find Coyol Restaurant. Most people arrive either by motorcycle or car, via a route that involves driving at least partially through a body of water at the base of the mountain. To say that it's difficult to get there would be an understatement – yet, once they arrive, people rarely complain.

Perched on the edge of a mountain, the restaurant overlooks the valley below and is famous for striking sunsets that can be watched from a swing. Most afternoons, the clouds move over the mountains and rush up the valley and into the restaurant and surrounding garden.

Before the local airport was built, the small village of Nosara was pretty hard to reach. Yet, because of the area's eco-friendly, all-natural and organic lifestyle, plus its surfing and beaches, travelers first started coming here in the late sixties. And, although the surfer crowd has largely been replaced by small boutique hotels and new restaurants that have opened in the past few years, the area's natural beauty remains its primary draw.

The once-sleepy yet still laid-back beach town is protected, with businesses limited from building directly on the beach and many regulations in place to protect sea turtles and other exotic animals that inhabit the nearby Ostional Wildlife Refuge. Environmental awareness and preservation have been cornerstones of Costa Rica's development since the seventies, and around 30% of its land and marine resources are currently protected – it's one of the first countries in the world to reach this target. The nation is now almost entirely powered by renewable sources and its current goal is to be the world's first carbon-neutral country.

Today, Nosara is home to plenty of yoga retreats, day spas, natural healing classes and a food scene that emphasizes quality ingredients like farm-fresh produce and just-caught seafood.

Coyol opened in September 2019 and quickly gained a reputation as one of the area's best restaurants. 'Four years in the making, a lot of sweat and tears, and we are finally ready!' co-founder Angelina Peri announced on Instagram just ahead of the launch. She'd already been busy, building a farm on the other side of the property.

After growing up in her father's hotel, Angelina had always known that a career in hospitality would be part of her plan. 'I've always been in kitchens helping,' she says.

Given the remote location, it's not surprising that one of the biggest challenges for Angelina and her team is simply the basic logistics of running a restaurant. 'We only have a tiny kitchen and getting everything we need up here in the mountains can be tricky,' she says. Because of this, the farm-to-table concept is more of a lifeline than a selling point.

'We just wanted to be true to ourselves by doing something that we both love and enjoy – the rest comes after that,' says Angelina. 'We've done something with our hearts, building the way we [want] and serving what we [want].'

'I always liked the mountains because of the cooler climate and the views,' says Angelina *(above)*. 'So, 12 years ago, my husband and I bought the property and we built a sustainable farm and lived there. Then we found the land the restaurant is on and knew it would be the perfect spot. It was my husband's vision, initially: he designed it and we built it together.'

At Coyol, the concept of farm-to-table is taken seriously. 'We source things as [locally] as we can. Most things are grown behind us on our farm, from tomatoes to lettuce and kale, and our fish is all caught locally, too,' says Angelina, who was born and raised in Costa Rica.

'We source things as locally as we can. Most things are grown on our farm.'

'It's a melting pot of both of us together and our food.'

The menu at Coyol is eclectic, with influences coming from both Costa Rica and further afield.

'My husband is Israeli, so there's some of that in there, and there's a mix of my family's heritage, which is Greek and English,' Angelina explains. 'So it's sort of a melting pot of both of us together and our food – that's the style of the place. Nothing is on the menu unless it's loved and tried and tested.'

Dishes change regularly based on what produce is available, but the menu could include smoked oysters, tuna tartare with mango and avocado or slow-cooked pork ribs marinated in a house blend of spices.

ŌSHADI

A regenerative farming, textile and fashion initiative.

Growing up in Erode, a major textile hub in India, gravitating towards the fabric industry came naturally to Nishanth Chopra. Friends, family – really, most people around him – had something to do with textiles. But the environmental impact didn't sit right with him.

When Nishanth returned to his hometown around 2014 after studying business in England, he decided to do something about it. The conventional way of making textiles was so 'mechanized and polluting', he says, and it dawned on him that it was better to tackle the problem head on than to complain about it.

So, Nishanth launched Ōshadi in 2016. The name comes from a Sanskrit word, which means 'essence of nature' or 'healing plant'. Ōshadi is a 'seed-to-sew' fashion brand and it works directly with cotton farmers to ensure that the materials being manufactured aren't harmful to the environment.

In the fashion industry, that's much easier said than done. When Nishanth started the brand and began looking into issues surrounding sustainable production, he found that things weren't as 'conscious' – an industry buzzword – and thoughtful as he'd hoped. This led to Ōshadi figuring out its own dyeing techniques. The brand also sourced the yarn and got it handwoven, working with a diverse cluster of craftsmen across India – ranging from Kashmir to Gujarat and Kolkata.

'I realized [that] the real impact would be when we work with a small cluster and grow with them consistently over a period of years and see the impact that way,' says Nishanth. 'If we keep working with different clusters each and every time, it doesn't create impact.'

Another major tipping point for Ōshadi came in 2018, when it displayed its collection in Paris. Nishanth met many like-minded designers who were looking for organic fabrics, leading to Ōshadi making and supplying textiles to them. Around the same time, Ōshadi collaborated on a project with fashion label Stella McCartney as part of The Commonwealth Fashion Exchange, which brought the Indian company a lot of attention. 'We got a lot of traction and a lot of new interest. And then [we] kind of evolved from mostly doing a collection to [being] a collective,' he says.

Then, in 2019, as everything was falling into place, Nishanth added the final missing piece: the source of the fibers. So, after dabbling with fashion and fabric, Ōshadi ventured into farming. With support from a US-based non-profit called Fibershed, Ōshadi started its seed-to-sew initiative of regenerative farming, where brands could come on board and connect straight to the farmers. '[We would] take care of all the puzzles in between, from farming to spinning, weaving, dyeing [and] sewing, all within 100 kilometers,' says Nishanth.

For Nishanth, Ōshadi is more than a business. 'Everyone's interconnected and we all have an obligation to live in harmony and live in tandem with each other,' he says. 'So, why do we destroy things and not choose the path of mindfulness?'

Ōshadi started with
a five-acre plot and
now has 50 acres – and
Nishanth *(above)* hopes
to expand to 1,000 acres
in the next five years. For
him, it's not just about
the expansion, but about
maintaining the brand's
values as it moves forward.

'I think it's profound – at
a very small level, we've
managed to really have an
impact in a very small way
but, as we grow gradually,
it would be nice to stay the
same, in terms of values
and fundamentals.'

As Ōshadi expands its farming initiatives, Nishanth expects further advantages. As they grow, the villages the brand collaborates with will be able to start working on autopilot, allowing Ōshadi to focus on not just sustainable farming but also on reforestation planning and ways to take care of local bodies of water.

'We realized that even the organic cotton we got was not farmed in a sustainable way – even though it was grown without pesticides [which certifies it as organic], it didn't ensure that everyone within the supply chain was paid well, from the farmers to the weavers to the spinners,' says Nishanth.

Financial help from Fibershed gave him the chance to grow his own cotton – and from there, he developed pest control using indigenous plants and creates his own compost. 'It was really organic. We simply found out what was wrong and then developed a solution,' he says.

'We found out what was wrong and developed a solution.'

TRUCK

A handcrafted furniture workshop (plus donut and coffee shop).

Tokuhiko Kise is adamant that he's not a businessman. Nor, he says, is he an artist. He's just a furniture maker. But this description is a little misleading because, over the past 26 years or so, Tokuhiko, or Tok, has built his company TRUCK from a creative passion project with zero customers into one of Japan's most beloved and most respected furniture brands.

It all began with his love of the outdoors. Growing up in Osaka, Tok would often hop on the back of his older brother's motorcycle as they explored the nearby mountains together. When he was 17, his desire to be closer to nature drew him to the city of Nagano, where he enrolled in a school to learn furniture-making. 'Part of me thought making furniture would be fun,' he says, 'but the other part thought that Nagano was just such a beautiful city, surrounded by beautiful mountains.'

Tok returned to Osaka a year later and, after working at a chair company near his parents' house, he rented a small shed, bought some old machines and opened his first wood shop at the age of 23.

Being his own boss was certainly rewarding, but there were a few early challenges. One was money. He'd spent most of his cash opening the wood shop, so Tok had little left to buy timber for his furniture and resorted to salvaging wood scraps on the street. Customers were another challenge – there weren't many. His location on the outskirts of the city meant that foot traffic was low and sales were few and far between.

Tok and his partner Hiromi Karatsu came up with a grand plan. They would move to Osaka proper and build an urban live-work space that was pretty revolutionary for the furniture industry at the time: a single place where they could make furniture, sell it to customers and live, too.

In 1997, they turned their dream into a reality and opened TRUCK. The idea was to create a shop and a brand that made long-lasting, timeless furniture that didn't follow trends. Its handcrafted pieces would look just as beautiful and sturdy decades in the future as they did on the day they were purchased. The furniture wouldn't be Scandi or farmhouse chic or mid-century modern – just TRUCK. One of its first collections highlighted the knots, cracks and rough textures in its wood, creating something beautiful from something that's traditionally perceived as a flaw.

Tok avoids wholesale, despite its potential to be a lucrative revenue stream, because it would mean him losing control. And he hates planning too far ahead into the future: 'My father always told me to make a five-year plan, but I live day by day,' he says. 'Well, maybe just for tomorrow.'

His most recent project has involved renting a spacious, industrial-style loft in downtown Los Angeles, which has slowly morphed from simply being a place to stay when he's in town to a showroom for his US clients. That wasn't really his intention – it's just what happened naturally.

And the best part of running TRUCK? 'I always say that I'm lucky because I get to do what I want to do and make what I want to make,' Tok says. 'It's that simple.'

One early success for TRUCK was Tok's idea to print 2,000 copies of a special product catalog and sell them in bookstores across Japan. The catalog quickly became a cult item that's since been referenced by a generation of Japanese creatives, despite Tok *(opposite)* and Hiromi doing everything themselves without any help from professional creatives – an approach that they also took when it came to building and designing their store and workshop.

'For 20 years after that, I'd meet photographers, stylists and designers who'd all have that first book,' Tok says. 'It was very funny, because we didn't know anything about commercial stuff at all. I just did what I wanted to do.'

This has been a central theme in Tok's career. He tends to follow his gut and doesn't pay much attention to external pressures or opinions. Today, Tok is still making it up as he goes along. And he's all the more successful for it.

'I always say I'm lucky because I get to do what I want and make what I want. It's that simple.'

As well as TRUCK, there's also Tok's Osaka-based donut and coffee shop, Bird, which he opened as a side project in 2009. The idea was for TRUCK customers to have a place to relax. But, unsurprisingly, Bird has spun off into its own successful brand: 'These days most Bird customers don't even know about TRUCK,' he says. 'I'm always like: What? It's right next door!'

Tok and Hiromi first encountered a donut machine while on a trip to Australia and immediately became fascinated with the process. Bird's donuts are made with quality ingredients, from free-range eggs to carefully selected wheat from Hokkaido and Okinawan salt.

All of the furniture in the cafe is from TRUCK, so customers can test out products while they relax. There's also a wood-burning stove that people can warm up by in the winter, which is fueled by scrap wood from the workshop.

OLI DE L'OLIVETA

Small-batch olive oil from a family's countryside home.

Nuria Val and Coke Bartrina run Oli de L'Oliveta, an olive-oil brand based in rural Catalonia, Spain. They found the abandoned olive grove a few years ago while exploring the area and saw a chance to create something outside of the city life of Barcelona, where they lived. They built a home on the land and, alongside a team of local farmers, worked to regenerate the soil and bring the neglected olive trees back to health. It took time and hard work, but it's now an escape for the family, who live between the city and the countryside. The couple had their first harvest two years after discovering the land and formed their brand, Oli de L'Oliveta.

'We produce only very small batches, which all depend on how much the trees want to produce in every given year,' says Coke. The business runs alongside the couple's other creative pursuits, with Nuria working as a model and both of them as photographers. 'The olive trees need very little care during the year, so it's something we can combine with our professional life,' says Coke. Nuria also runs a plant-based beauty brand called ROWSE.

There are around 1,500kg of olives in a normal harvest every autumn, once the fruit has ripened after a summer in Spain's sunshine. This makes 150 liters of olive oil that's processed nearby, which is decanted into metal cans, 'the best way to preserve the flavor of the oil', according to Coke.

Some are given to friends, family and neighbors, while others find their way into kitchens around the world.

Neither Nuria nor Coke were immersed in the world of olive oil before they bought the land. 'We had to learn everything from scratch, so we attended some olive-oil tasting classes, which were accompanied by reading books,' says Coke. 'It was hard work to bring the land back to the point of producing fruit and oil, but it feels amazing to see the olive trees healthy.'

As can happen with any business that brings together the unpredictable elements of nature and family, last year there was no olive harvest at all as there was a record heatwave in the region – which happened to coincide with the birth of the couple's daughter, Olivia. 'The heatwave was a direct consequence of climate change – the hot weather is arriving earlier in the year than ever,' says Coke.

'We're looking forward to a great harvest this year. Our daughter is the happiest kid when we're here. She just started walking a couple of weeks ago and she loves touching the plants with her small hands and seeing all the animals that hang around the property.'

Living and working in such a naturally beautiful part of the world has had a huge effect on the couple, spurring a conscious decision for them to balance their life in Barcelona with living somewhere so rural. 'Nuria and I have always been very inspired by nature and being there feels like having a small piece of heaven,' says Coke. 'All the senses awaken, everything moves slower, the birds singing fill your ears and the smell of rosemary pops up every time you walk around the farm.'

'Making tasty olive oil for our friends, family and customers is what we want to do,' says Coke. The couple's loved ones help harvest the olives each autumn over four days before it's pressed and bottled locally.

The couple say that olive oil is used in almost every meal they cook, often paired with local meat and cheese. Described as tasting like 'fresh vegetables and flowers', it's a reflection of the place where it's produced.

'Our only goal is to share with people and recover part of the money that goes into making it.'

'Being there feels like having a small piece of heaven. All the senses awaken.'

When the couple first saw the land, it was in complete ruin. There was an abandoned old house, but they saw its potential. Fitting in with the traditional architecture of the area, the white-washed exterior protects the house from the increasingly hot summers. Finished with solar panels and rainwater tanks, it's been designed to fit with the same sustainable ethos as the oil they produce.

'The design of the house was aesthetically inspired by the old farming sheds of the area. We designed it in collaboration with Barcelona interiors studio Conti, Cert, with locally sourced materials,' says Coke. 'We're completely off-grid here, so we've tried to make it as efficient as possible.'

Coke built the furniture inside the house from wood found near the property. Catalan-style tiles can be found throughout, as well as an abundance of local wildflowers in ceramics.

'Recently, Spain suffered from a heatwave. The flowers got damaged before being pollinated, so we had almost no olives.'

'Recently, Spain suffered from a heatwave that struck just when the olive trees were in bloom. The [flowers] got damaged before being pollinated, so we had almost no olives. It [wasn't] worth harvesting them since there's a minimum required to be able to bring them to the mill,' says Coke.

A range of factors are impacting olive harvests around the world, so the efforts of small producers to protect the process will be an important part of the future.

FOOD AND DRINK

Opening a food-and-drink business is notoriously tough – and that hasn't changed in recent years. But the opportunities are limitless.

Why the food industry is more creative than ever

Despite the challenges involved in setting up and staying afloat, the food-and-drink industry has some of most exciting opportunities and plenty of potential for change. From the rise of chef-artists to three areas to keep an eye out for, here's a brief guide to the sector.

The co-founders of London restaurant group BAO, Erchen Chang and Shing Tat Chung *(left)*, demonstrate the potential for a design-led food brand.

Egypt-born artist Laila Gohar has harnessed her creativity with food to launch her own tableware brand called Gohar World *(right)*.

Conventional wisdom tells us not to play with our food. Don't touch it. Don't move it around. Don't do anything other than eat it. Yet rules are made to be broken. And break them we do.

Food has become as much an art as it is a craft, and playing with it has become an industry unto itself. Largely thanks to social media and our extremely online culture, no longer is opening a restaurant one of the only – very expensive – ways into the industry.

If you've been online recently, chances are you've come across images of meringue swans, pastry peacocks, bras made from oranges, translucent champagne jellyfish with flowers inside, giant butter sculptures, tattooed baby potatoes. The list goes on. Across social media, they're everywhere: outrageously brilliant and intricate creations made using food, all so perfect it's never clear whether they're even edible.

Creative food styling has never been in higher demand, with luxury brands increasingly tapping chefs, food artists and set designers to turn the act of feeding a crowd into a multidimensional experience. Over-the-top banquets and menus for which the consumption of the food isn't really the point go viral almost every day.

Engaging audiences using food and visual storytelling has turned into big business. Cheap technology has made content creators of us all. It's never been easier to make, reproduce, publish and edit images and videos online. The more your image is liked and shared, the more value generated for the platform it was posted on, for the advertiser and, most likely, for the influencer, too. Abundance over scarcity is the goal.

Laila Gohar was quick to take advantage of this. Born in Cairo, she moved to the US for university and gradually started working in restaurants. On the side, she grew a catering business called Sunday Supper. Magazine parties and brand-sponsored events were plentiful, but Laila didn't start moving in a more subversive, surrealist direction until about 2016.

By then she'd ditched Sunday Supper and her creations were exploding in scale and ingenuity, bringing the worlds of art, design, fashion and food closer together than ever before. Building momentum largely through her Instagram

account (*@lailacooks*), she frequently posts things like the giant prawn pyramids she made for fashion label Ganni or the mountain of 5,000 marshmallows she produced for luxury jewelry brand Tiffany. At the events, like night follows day, guests post pictures on Instagram and tag the brands, as well as Laila. Everyone's a winner.

Today, with more than 260,000 Instagram followers, she remains one of the leading chef-artists in the world. According to a recent profile of her in The New Yorker, when Laila was a guest at a dinner hosted by Nike in 2020, Drake introduced her as the Björk of food. Later that year, she and her sister, Nadia, launched Gohar World, a tableware brand described as 'a place where adults wear lace bibs, cauliflowers are candles, and every plate comes with beans'.

More than anyone else, Laila symbolizes the new wave of culinary-focused art brands that are blowing up across social media, as well as dominating art, fashion and design parties, gallery openings and events all around the world. Big brands can't get enough of it, making it a potentially lucrative career.

Another example is Gab Bois (*@gabbois*), an artist from Montreal, Canada, who frequently uses food in unusual ways. The most striking pieces that she's posted to her almost 700,000 Instagram followers include blueberry jewelry, cotton-candy panties and a bra made out of eggs (sunny side up), as well as furniture that's a literal representation of comfort food, like her pasta-dough sofa with ravioli pillows. From beauty brand Glossier to car manufacturer Mercedes-Benz, her client list reveals the cross-industry appeal of her work.

Japanese artist Daisuke (*@dimda_*) has a similarly whimsical aesthetic – bread Crocs, a popcorn tie, a mini bedroom made from sushi – that has seen him work with the likes of fashion brands Hermès, Prada and Puma among others.

All of these chef-artists point to the widely held acceptance that we no longer need Michelin-starred restaurants to have memorable experiences with food. If anything, we're moving away from these spaces, as more creatively minded individuals find new, innovative ways to play around with what's served on a plate.

Learnings along the way

Looking back on the brands they've built, we asked three business owners about some of the things they've learned on their journey.

Keegan Fong, Woon Kitchen

Based in Los Angeles' Historic Filipinotown, Woon Kitchen is a family-run Chinese restaurant that serves Shanghainese- and Cantonese-style food to its community of devoted fans. With just a handful of items on the menu, founder Keegan Fong wanted to bring elements of his mom's cooking and hospitality to the space. Keegan's opening a site in Pasadena soon.

Keegan:
'Woon is very much a reflection of my upbringing. I'd never worked in the restaurant industry before opening this place, but I knew I wanted to do something that revolved around my mom's dream of having her own restaurant. Growing up, it felt like our family kitchen was sort of that – it was always open to my friends, and there was always food. Opening a restaurant felt like the biggest challenge and probably the dumbest thing to do, but that's kind of how it all came about. I was never like: let's make Woon a community hub – but it [has], in many ways, become just that. I wanted other people to be a part of it.

'In my past life in marketing, I made a lot of connections and, to some extent, I wanted to bring a lot of them along for the ride – if they wanted to be a part of it. And that's where the brand aspect comes in. It was through using the space as a community hub. It just kind of organically happened and, suddenly, with Woon, we were hosting a lot – hosting other concepts and pop-ups within our space, because that's how *we* got off the ground. I think Covid had a lot to do with it, too, in that as we emerged out of it, we wanted to bring people back together as much as we could.'

'We wanted to bring people back together as much as we could.'

Shing Tat Chung, BAO

Back in 2013, BAO launched as a street-food stall and quickly went about popularizing steamed Taiwanese buns in the UK. It moved to its first permanent London restaurant in 2015, and today it has six sites dotted around the city, as well as its own app. Its co-founders, Shing Tat Chung, Erchen Chang and Wai Ting Chung, also published a cookbook in 2022, which is equal parts memoir and recipes from the restaurants.

Shing:
'During the pandemic, everyone took the hit and BAO wasn't immune to it. We had some dark moments. In 2022, we had to close one of our sites [in Fitzrovia]. That was very sad for us. But we had to think innovatively and make adjustments pretty fast. Things have turned and we're doing really well. Either way, we're staying prudent. We're staying nimble.

'Sticking with one site – we'd question what we were doing. [We] may as well step back and go to the beach. We're driven by creating restaurants and growing our mission – to educate around Taiwanese food. So, even though it's definitely more complex growing a food business beyond one site, it's something we felt like we had to do.

'We want to create a company where people want to grow with us and stay for their career. So, we put together a strategy of how we tackle this. We stepped back and started from scratch. We looked at how we hire and motivate our staff, how we get the culture right, how we get pipelines into senior positions right. Most people don't see hospitality as a long-term career choice. But we always wanted to create the right conditions to change that. We did a 360 review.

'Hospitality comes with a lot of noise. It's relentless. Even so, we're always looking for the next idea.'

'Community is at the heart of what we do, so being able to be a part of people's lives in this area is key to growing our business.'

Tom Pye, Good Ways Deli

Old-school but inventive sandwiches and nostalgic desserts, all made with indigenous Australian ingredients, are the backbone of Good Ways Deli in Sydney. Founded by Tom Pye and Jordan McKenzie in 2021, the brand opened its first deli in the district of Redfern, which was shortly followed by a second site in the nearby suburb of Alexandria.

Tom:
'Dream big. That's what I wish we knew when we started. We were conservative when we first opened and really underestimated the scale of what we'd sell and the success of our first site in Redfern. We opened in 2021 amid the pandemic and, by the following year, we needed to open our second site in Alexandria and completely reconfigure our Redfern kitchen to keep up with the demand [for] the bread we bake fresh each morning.

'Community is at the heart of what we do, so being able to be a part of people's lives in this area is key to growing our business.'

Trend report

The food-and-drink industry has a lot of opportunities when it comes to investment and innovation. After all, is there another sector that affects as many people from various backgrounds all around the world? In the hands of the right people, it also has the potential to solve environmental and social problems. Here, experts and business owners spotlight three areas to look out for.

Upcycling food

'Reduce, reuse, recycle' is a slogan that's been drilled into us since the inception of the environmental movement in the seventies. Yet, in so far as it applied to food at all, it applied to the packaging. Only in more recent years has the idea of reducing, reusing and recycling food come to prominence in the media and the food industry. You could argue that the concept isn't new, but it's one that our ancestors would have lived by instinctively. But credit where credit's due: pioneering food brands like Toast, Rubies in the Rubble, Black Cow Vodka and ReGrained are transforming the by-products of commercial food production into something edible or usable and, in doing so, showing the global industry that it's throwing money away.

And lots of it, according to Chloë Stewart of food brand Nibs Etc, whose granola and snacks are made with fruit and vegetable pulp from cider and juice presses in England. 'The upcycled [food] industry is valued at $46 billion, so I'd definitely encourage people to go into it,' she says. 'I'm one small business trying to shout about it but, if there are several voices, we're louder and, if bigger companies understand the financial and sustainable benefits of doing it, then it'll become mainstream.'

There are many new ideas, but there are also plenty of existing bandwagons worth jumping on – as the co-existence of Toast and Crumbs Brewing, two brands brewing beer from waste bread, shows. 'Bread is the second-most-wasted food in households – 44% of bread never gets eaten,' says Morgan Arnell, co-founder of Crumbs. 'If some of the bigger brewers replaced 5% of their malt with breadcrumbs – which are surprisingly efficient in the fermentation – it'd make a massive difference.' Brewing with bread dates back to pre-Egyptian times – it's not new, by any means. 'I'd love to see the day when we stop talking about food waste and start talking about food resource,' Chloë says.

Great grains

There's huge potential in the cereals industry. During the Green Revolution of the 20th century, thousands of grains around the world were replaced with a handful of modern varieties, genetically bred to be fast-growing and high-yielding. But they proved unsustainable, with short stems and shallow roots that rendered them more dependent on carbon-intensive chemical fertilizers, pesticides and herbicides.

Soil erosion, disease outbreaks and the decline of pollinators have since followed, compounded by climate change. This has laid the groundwork for a return to regional or heritage varieties. One of the forerunners in this space is Hodmedod's, a business that supports British farmers to grow these varieties.

'We know that climate change poses a real threat to food production, that using poisons [pesticides] to effect a short-term fix is having a big impact on insect populations and the huge threat to climate pressure that synthetic nitrogen brings,' explains Hodmedod's co-founder Josiah Meldrum. 'What we need are diverse, adaptive crops that are rich in flavor and nutrients, and we need them not to be a niche, but something tens of thousands of farmers are growing worldwide.'

At Talgarth Mill in the UK's Brecon Beacons National Park, the team mill their own flour and transform it into bara brith, a Welsh bread. Pollen Bakery in Manchester creates old-fashioned porridge loaves, while at other bakeries across the UK, regional bakes like bannocks, farls and Staffordshire oatcakes are being rediscovered along with the grains they're based on.

London-based Wildfarmed is working to get its sustainably farmed flour into larger operations, as well as into independent retailers. It doesn't exclusively focus on heritage grains, because it's trying to convince farmers to adopt sustainable systems at scale and speed.

'We need to transition as much land out of chemical systems into biological systems as possible,' says Wildfarmed's co-founder George Lamb. 'We have to hope that, as environmental literacy rises, customers will demand better, and smart businesses will cater for that.'

'As environmental literacy rises, customers will demand better, and smart businesses will cater for that.'

Going global

'All successful brands are the result of successful storytelling.'

There's no doubt that more and more people are drawing on the flavors of their heritages for recipes, restaurants, meal kits and other businesses – but should this really be classed as a trend?

'It's a strange thing to call a trend,' says Gurdeep Loyal, food-and-drink consultant and author of Mother Tongue: Flavours of a Second Generation. 'It's the same as talking about certain cuisines as a trend. You're reflecting a western lens on it, rather than saying you've discovered what's always been there and [something] that's not static, but constantly evolving.'

Peruvian, West African, Sri Lankan, Norwegian – 'these cuisines are alive, and what excites me is that people of those diasporas are owning their culinary narratives and telling their story,' he continues. There are different people doing different things within similar culinary contexts – a perspective that holds far more interest for businesses and customers.

This is evident in the books we buy, the ingredients we scour the shelves for and the rapid rise of cookery courses. UK-based Oma Kitchen is one such course, established by Hugo Lakin and David Reed. It offers online learning, video tutorials and all non-perishable ingredients for dishes from Korea, Mexico and North India.

Food consultant and writer Mallika Basu works with businesses to help them incorporate recipes and ingredients that draw upon international cuisines, paying careful attention to regionality. 'You don't want only a limited, traditional use for [an] ingredient, if you want to create a market for it. You want creative uses and you want it to be friendly to use,' she says.

When working with flavors and dishes drawn from a cuisine other than your own, it's important to 'speak to the right people, showcase their expertise and continue to champion that in a symbiotic relationship. Calling upon that expertise then failing to acknowledge [it] is where brands go wrong,' she says.

'All successful brands are the result of successful storytelling. Figuring out how to tell your story, or enabling someone else's story to be told without twisting the narrative to suit your agenda, creates a much more valuable brand in the long run,' says Gurdeep.

Hugo Lakin *(left)* and David Reed *(right)* launched Oma Kitchen in 2020. To create their lessons, they consult leading voices, recipe writers, chefs, producers and more.

LA BANCHINA

A harborside restaurant and sauna.

Four times a year, Christer Bredgaard would drive down from Denmark to Italy, pack his van full of wine and charcuterie, and then head back up north. Back then, he was working as a cabinet maker, running a small wine importing business on the side but, over time, the wine imports almost unintentionally morphed into his first restaurant, Il Buco.

'I had some food from this opening party that I'd forgotten to serve, so I invited some friends to dinner. Then came more friends and I started to charge a little money. Suddenly, I had this very popular supper club in Copenhagen. It just grew and transformed slowly until I had a big restaurant and a lot of employees,' Christer explains.

In 2015, a mutual friend tried (and failed) to launch a cafe in a rejuvenated corner of Copenhagen's former industrial dockyard neighborhood, Refshaleøen. He turned to Christer for help – maybe they could try again? But Christer doesn't like going into business with other people; he's seen first hand with close friends how often it can end in tears – or a courtroom. He declined the offer.

A few months later, however, the friend asked if he wanted to take the contract off his hands. On that plot of land now sits La Banchina, a 14-seat restaurant with its own swimming dock and sauna. It's the perfect sanctuary for when long Scandinavian winter nights are swapped for light-filled summer days. Because of its latitude, Copenhagen gets more than 17 hours of daylight during the summer months. And, for around six weeks each year, temperatures can rise to 25°C, turning the Danish capital into a quasi-Mediterranean idyll.

'When I started, there was only one restaurant out [in this area],' says Christer. Then came a sprawling street-food market called Reffen, seasonal bakery Lille and two-Michelin-starred restaurant Alchemist. Now Refshaleøen is connected to the rest of the city by electric ferries, known as harbor buses, which bring locals across the main canal. Safe to say, footfall has increased significantly since La Banchina opened its doors in 2016.

People can while away whole days at La Banchina. From 8am, people do yoga on the dock. The menu, like the name – meaning 'pier' in Italian – is inspired by Italy, but is resolutely Danish, using Danish ingredients. In winter, you'll find a hearty leek soup with a cheesy mushroom toast. In spring, grilled asparagus with smoked crème fraîche.

There are only ever four dishes on the menu. This means Christer can dedicate time to his other restaurant, which can be a little more demanding. But he's built a strong enough team around him, so he usually spends three weeks in Los Angeles for his birthday in January – the only other place where he feels 'at home', he says.

But there's a twist in the tale: Christer's contract for La Banchina ends in 2025. 'I hope I can get three, four or five years extra. But we have a limited life out here because they're developing,' he says. 'But I knew that from the very beginning. That's just a part of the deal. We just want to enjoy it while it's still here.'

For Christer, nothing beats the magic of a summer's day at La Banchina. 'If I end up out there with a couple of friends and we have some cold beers and watch the sunset while people are swimming and having a good time – it just adds up in a more special way,' he says.

Of course, it's not all sunsets and rainbows. Covid was a 'pain in the ass', notes Christer, and La Banchina didn't escape the post-pandemic labor shortages and cost increases that took a chunk out of the global hospitality industry.

'Watch the sunset while people are swimming and having a good time – it adds up in a special way.'

Not many restaurants can boast their own wood-fired sauna, but La Banchina's has room for up to eight people. The sauna is a necessity during the winter months to warm those Danes hardy enough to plunge into the canal. In typically laid-back Danish style, swimwear in the sauna is optional.

In the summer months, locals flock to the water, often swimming in the canals that cut through the center of Copenhagen. 'It seems like people are starving to get out and drink wine,' says Christer.

If you don't manage to grab a seat inside at La Banchina, the pier becomes your table, where you can lunch cross-legged to the sound of lapping water. Copenhagen frequently wins awards for its cleanliness, thanks to enormous investment from the city municipality stretching back to the 2000s. In 2002, the first public harbor opened in the area of Islands Brygge, and the rest is history.

SENSE OF SELF

A bathhouse and wellness center in an old print foundry.

◉ MELBOURNE, AUSTRALIA

A tranquil, incense-filled bathhouse might be the last thing you'd expect to find down an inner-city street in Melbourne, yet it's just the sort of escape that Mary Minas and Freya Berwick wanted it to be. With everything from an ice bath, steam room and sauna to a heated pool and wellness center filled with plants, books and snacks, Sense of Self has become a cornerstone of its community.

Situated in an old print foundry in Collingwood, from the street Sense of Self looks entirely unassuming. Step inside, though, and a dreamlike atmosphere comes alive. Upstairs are massage studios draped with heavy linen curtains where guests can choose from in-house mixed blends of essential oils for their treatment. The bathhouse below begins with a suite of gender-neutral change rooms that are a key part of the business' ethos.

Sense of Self is split into quiet and social hours to best allow guests to experience the space as they wish. 'It was super intentional; we wanted people to be able to have this element of social connection, so you can come and do your own thing or come to hang out with people,' says Mary. 'Even before the pandemic, there was a loneliness epidemic and so, when we were designing the space, we wanted there to be lots of spots for people to come together.'

The idea to launch the business came from a chance meeting on a Master of Entrepreneurship course at The University of Melbourne. 'Mary came into that course wanting to do something around bathhouses and bathing, and I came in wanting to do something about hotels. By the end of the course, we came together on Sense of Self,' Freya explains.

Prior to meeting, Mary was a producer working in the Australian film industry before moving to London to work with Ridley Scott's production company, Scott Free, where she developed scripts. 'While I was there, I started researching bathhouses throughout the ages for a documentary that I wanted to make. I went to about 40 bathhouses around the world, interviewed owners, learned about the different traditions and business models. But, by the end of it, I realized I didn't want to make a doco about it – I wanted to run one,' says Mary.

Freya, on the other hand, worked in botanical science, which led her to Norway where she switched paths and started redeveloping a hotel in the western fjords. 'I loved living in this really small place, it was a beautiful experience. I got obsessed with the contrast of bathing, in particular, jumping from the sauna into cold bodies of water,' says Freya. It was no surprise once Mary and Freya met that their concept for Sense of Self was born.

Launching a bathhouse after the pandemic put many different elements of safety into the equation. However, it also gave them the time they needed to make this a perfect 'post-pandemic space' with air filtration and space for distancing.

'There were a few times when we really thought people would never be able to come together in a place like this again, but the opposite has happened – there's been such a craving and a desire for people to actually be together,' says Freya.

It was a chance meeting on a business course that led to Mary *(left)* and Freya *(right)* connecting. Despite coming from pretty different career backgrounds, they bonded over their love of spas.

Entering Sense of Self from the busy industrial-looking street in Collingwood is a total shift in atmosphere. An area of central Melbourne, Collingwood is full of old workers' cottages, converted warehouses and is a hub of the creative industry in the city.

The light-filled lobby is stocked with a curated selection of swimwear, beauty products and fragrances all for customers to continue their experience beyond the spa.

Once guests arrive, they're asked to leave their phones in the lockers and commit to an offline experience while in the space.

'The two of us coming together strengthened all the ideas we had.'

Sense of Self opened in March 2021, one year after Melbourne's first Covid lockdown. 'Building something as technical as a spa, steam room or sauna is difficult at the best of times. But trying to do it when there were so many restrictions was almost impossible,' says Mary.

'It took a few years to get it off the ground, but the two of us coming together really strengthened all the ideas we had. We spent a few years building a community audience, developing our understanding of what we wanted and then we really needed to get finance, as it's not the sort of business you can build with no money.'

Inside each changing room is a simple sign with a list of bathing basics that include 'stay hydrated' and 'no hanky panky'. The whole space is gender-neutral and changing rooms are split between a large communal space and separate cubicles lined with linen curtains.

'One of the undergirding values is belonging; we want everyone to feel welcome and comfortable in this space and in their bodies,' says Mary.

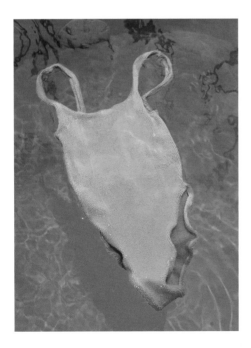

AGUA MÁGICA

A mezcal (and sometimes fashion) brand investing in its community.

At the beginning of his career, Rafael Shin never thought he'd be running a mezcal brand in Oaxaca. After all, one of his first jobs was in finance, working as an analyst at investment bank Morgan Stanley. But the best career paths don't always follow straight lines.

His parents left Seoul for Mexico just after he was born. 'They saw that the weather in Mexico was perfect, and they decided that it's where they wanted to raise their children,' Rafael explains. 'We were the 15th Korean family ever to live in the country.' Growing up in Mexico City, Rafael was heavily influenced by the area and the country's culture (his whole family was – his father jumped into Latin-American history studies almost straight away). In particular, he always liked mezcal and the culture that surrounds it.

After moving to New York to start his finance career, there were elements from Mexico that he missed. 'It's a place that I'd say is probably the richest culturally, but poorest economically, and I wanted to do something about it,' he says. While at Morgan Stanley, he worked as a consultant for global alcohol brands. 'My early career was connected to tequila and mezcal, but I had no experience in building a brand or creating a product,' he says.

Rafael knew he wanted to start a brand of mezcal – which is distilled from the heart of the agave plant – and spent years doing research, looking at everything from the exact locations where agave grows to the communities that would be involved in its production. In 2019, he walked away from the world of finance and started working on Agua Mágica full time. 'When you start something, especially as a first-time entrepreneur like myself, it gets a bit overwhelming because you have to make so many decisions that you don't know where to start,' he says.

'[Mezcal has] got mystical properties, I think,' Rafael says, explaining that Agua Mágica translates to 'magic water'. 'Not just health benefits – it's more spiritual. It's drunk at all big occasions in Mexico, from funerals to weddings. It's the same role that something like champagne has in some European countries. It's not just for getting drunk,' he says.

Agave plants can take around 25 years to mature and the skills needed to produce mezcal are very specific, from baking the *piñas* (the heart of the agave plant) to distillation. 'The price of our mezcal is set because it's extremely important for me to correctly pay the people involved in its production. I see them as entrepreneurs – they're small, independent producers who are highly skilled,' says Rafael. In addition, mezcal is highly regulated and can only be named as such if it adheres to a set of strict parameters, which include using 100% agave sourced exclusively from nine of Mexico's states, with no additives – making it a more premium product than many tequilas, which require a minimum of 51% agave content.

'There's no reason why Oaxaca shouldn't be seen in the same way as Burgundy or other wine regions in France,' he says. 'There's so much going on here and we're a single-origin product just like wine. I want people to taste the place.'

Rafael aims to center Agua Mágica as a new generation of premium mezcal producers that'll be able to change 'how Mexican culture is perceived worldwide', while also introducing new, global audiences to the spirit he's chosen to dedicate his life to. Plus, there are a few myths he hopes to dispel.

'Over the past two years, I think we've seen a feeling of positive surprise when [people] taste our mezcal because it's different from people's perceptions of what mezcal is,' he explains. 'Most of the mezcal that people have tried is mass-produced and super smoky and strong. When they taste ours, they say: "I didn't realize I liked mezcal!"'

'When people taste ours, they say: "I didn't realize I liked mezcal!"'

While Agua Mágica is still in its early stages as a business, its reputation for quality mezcal is growing. And the brand is expanding in unexpected ways, such as collaborations with leisurewear brand Tombolo on a collection of embroidered shirts, shorts and hats inspired by Oaxacan craftsmanship.

For Rafael, being bold is essential for anyone out there wanting to start something of their own. 'You'll never feel ready to start what you want to do,' he says. 'I come from finance, so I'm a naturally risk-averse person in general. But, when I think about it, I wish I'd just started this business earlier in my life, even though I didn't feel ready. You'll learn what you need to know as you go along. I think that it's one of those things, like when you go to a pool – instead of dipping your toes in, take the plunge and then figure it out.'

'The older I get, the more I think about how progressive the people here in Oaxaca are in terms of how they think about their connection to nature and community,' reflects Rafael. 'The land here is owned by the community – you can't just show up and buy a part of it because it belongs to everyone.' This sense of community is why it was important for Agua Mágica to source its agave from small farmers.

'Instead of dipping your toes in, take the plunge and then figure it out.'

OLD CARPET FACTORY

A recording studio and art residency on a car-free island.

On any given day, groups of artists and musicians step off the ferry from Athens onto the stone harbor steps of Hydra, a Greek island in the Aegean Sea. No cars are allowed here, so horses and mules will be waiting to transport them across a maze of cobbled streets to their destination.

Past lots of lemon trees and tavernas, there's a double door adorned with little more than a brass knocker. It doesn't look like much, but step inside and a creative sanctuary unfurls, known as the Old Carpet Factory.

Since 2015, the Old Carpet Factory, a recording studio and artist residency, has been welcoming traveling creatives to Hydra. As the name suggests, the area was once the site of a weaving school that made textiles and carpets. Aside from a few alterations, the villa dates back to the 18th century. With three bedrooms and a rooftop suite, there's space for up to eight guests at a time. For musicians, its stone interiors and high ceilings spell good news for the acoustics. For artists, the living room's three giant west-facing windows are perfect for letting in Greece's sublime light.

Life unfolds languidly at the Old Carpet Factory: coffee on the terrace overlooking the old town; gazing out across the bay while sitting at the 1924 Steinway & Sons piano. Last October, it took the best part of a day and the labor of 12 people to carry that piano through the narrow and sloping streets of Hydra. For once, the island's workhorses were supplanted – it was deemed necessary to prevent the instrument from going out of tune, and

especially important because the piano contains the signatures of all its tuners dating back to the thirties.

Owner and music producer Stephan Colloredo-Mansfeld – or Steph, as everyone calls him – has a deep attachment to Hydra. After all, he grew up there. Thanks to strict archaeological and building restrictions and the fact it's remained vehicle-free, the island hasn't changed much since his childhood, he says. In previous interviews, he's quoted American novelist Henry Miller, who visited the island in the thirties, as saying Hydra has 'this purity, this wild and naked perfection'; it's 'the very epitome of that flawless anarchy'. And that's just how he likes it.

The house is always filled with creative people, Steph says; it's a rare day when nobody is recording at the studio, making art or simply stopping by for a visit. Many artists have stayed over the years, from French musician Sébastien Tellier to Italian artist Margherita Chiarva. Steph summarizes the atmosphere of the place with the title of a novel written by Greek author Makis Malaféka, inspired by his stay at the villa: De Les Kouventa. Meaning? 'You don't say a word.'

With its patchy internet, light-filled rooms and plentiful bar hidden inside an antique cupboard, the Old Carpet Factory provides the requisite sustenance for traveling independent spirits. 'Preserving [the house's] authenticity while catering to present-day recording artists is a challenge,' he says. But the joy from overcoming those challenges is the reason why Steph continues to sustain his dream.

Steph's mother Kristina Colloredo-Mansfeld, a painter, bought the house in the seventies. She fell in love with it because of the living room's windows, which are the tallest on the island.

Hydra feels like a step back in time because the architecture of the island is protected – any new construction must be built in accordance with the architectural methods and style of the 18th century.

'My parents' generation and the one before them were true bohemians in the sense that they came to Hydra in search of creative freedom away from the industrial consumer society. They were also running away from the restricting norms of western societies,' says Steph. 'Dissidence, protest, eccentricity and excess became their lifestyle.'

The Old Carpet Factory has been a labor of love for Steph. He's converted the lower part of the house into a recording studio and has filled the place with instruments from all corners of the world.

You'll find a multitude of microphone boxes piled on top of drum kits, bongos and other rare instruments – including the theremin, an electronic instrument that's controlled without any physical contact from the performer.

Steph says that nostalgia was a powerful factor when he was conceptualizing the Old Carpet Factory. His aim was to build a sort of artists' colony, which could recreate the magical atmosphere of the bohemians and dropouts that he grew up surrounded by.

'There's a definite element of recreating my childhood, in combination with a lust and longing to create and fill certain voids from my upbringing,' he says.

'There's an element of recreating my childhood – a lust to fill certain voids.'

'Looking back at my upbringing on the island, one has to imagine a liberal hippy upbringing with few restrictions and limitations, which is exactly the freedom a creative person would look for,' says Steph. 'I'd like to believe that the Old Carpet Factory has become a place where anarchy and order meet, where artists can feel free without getting lost.'

You can only access Hydra, one of Greece's Saronic Islands, by boat. 'Hydra island, with its untouched rugged beauty, brings lots of artists, creatives and eccentrics together. And, by means of word of mouth, many end up staying at the house or visiting during their stay,' says Steph.

Lots of different types of people drop into Old Carpet Factory, helping the place retain its eccentricity. 'We never know who'll stop by on any given day.'

'Hydra island brings lots of artists, creatives and eccentrics together.'

DREAM TOOLKIT

You'll encounter a few challenges on your journey to setting up your dream business. Here are some tools to help.

What are some of the challenges of setting up your own dream business that people don't always talk about? How do you maintain a healthy work-life balance when you're working for yourself? And when's the right time to leave your regular job to launch your dream business? We put these three questions to the founders of a ramen shop, a ceramic tile studio and a comedy and food events company to find some workable solutions.

(PART ONE)

Setting up

As partners in Netherlands-based Studio GdB, childhood friends Gilles de Brock and Jaap Giesen design, create and sell ceramic tiles to clients all over the world. The foundation for these successes – besides the tiles' unique rich, striking patterns – has been years of hard work and graft, which are the foundations for any success as a business owner.

Starting your own business will always come with challenges. Not just paperwork, accounting and staffing, but also the mental hurdles. The self-doubt. The responsibility. The budgeting. It'll test even the most resilient, says Gilles.

'You have an idea and, of course, you believe in that idea. You think it's going to be something, but to really commit to that idea – that's a huge challenge,' he says.

MONEY TALKS

The more obvious problems are connected to money. Setting up a business isn't cheap and it can be difficult to cover the initial costs, particularly if you require stock, equipment or a physical premise, such as when you're opening a restaurant.

Shivas Howard-Brown, founder of London-based Friendly Pressure, which sources, refurbishes and customizes heritage audio systems, bought his first speakers using a short-term government loan. He also borrowed money from his friends. 'At some point, you have to forget your ego,' he says.

Luke Findlay, co-founder of Supa Ya Ramen, which has two sites in London that serve 'traditionally inauthentic' flavors, found the

£15,000 required to kit out his first restaurant through his family, who he sold some equity to. But, even then, he had to beg suppliers to service him on account. 'We were basically scribbling around for people to give us stuff,' he recalls.

Even if you're fortunate enough to have savings, it can be hard to know how much to invest. Gilles launched Studio GdB using money he'd put aside to buy his first home. 'There was a huge financial risk to it,' he says.

STICK TO THE BUDGET

Even after you've established the basics of your business, you'll probably still need to cut back on spending – partly because you'll never know when the next paycheck is coming, but also because you'll likely need to reinvest some of your profits in the business. Gilles, for this reason, moved into his mother's home, which was empty. 'Looking back now, it's ridiculous how little income I survived on at the time,' he says. 'That's not normal for any grown man.'

To preserve funds, Shivas drastically limited his vacations and nights out; instead, he'd do yoga videos at home and go on long cycling trips, because they were free. 'Your outgoings must come down if you want to find the money to invest in the new setup,' he says. 'You've got to sacrifice parts of your lifestyle,' he says.

Some of this, of course, might pose practical problems – if, say, you have a mortgage or dependents. But the effects might be more psychological, eroding your pride and your feeling of self-worth, while you'll likely feel stressed about not having a steady income.

CHANGE YOUR MINDSET

Not that all this is a bad thing, though, according to Shivas. 'Consistency and stability is great, but it doesn't work in an entrepreneurial setting,' he says. 'Constantly being on the edge is going to make you push yourself harder and further.'

And, from his experience, he's come to crave the rewards of progress. 'Within a month, if you spend time away from socializing, you'll get double the amount of rewards – like two more clients or six more meetings for potential gigs,' he says. 'That's the lifeblood that gives you the energy to pour more time into it.'

To help overcome those feelings of financial insecurity, he suggests focusing on the process rather than the end goal. 'Focusing on day by day, week by week is the key,' he adds. 'If you're constantly focused on doing what you're doing to a high standard, I think the money will come.'

There might also be other psychological implications of setting up your own business, says Rhiannon Butler, one half of London-based

'Focusing on day by day, week by week is the key.'

Studio GdB built a machine that could 'print' custom ceramic tiles.

Mam Sham, which stages immersive dining experiences across the city. 'You've got all the financial stuff – like not knowing how your next launch is going to go or when your next event is gonna be – but there are quite a lot of mental challenges that come with it [too].'

One of the more difficult parts is not being able to plan. 'You always want to be free and available for the next opportunity because, when it's your own business, you care so much,' she says. 'When friends are like, "We should do something in June," we're like: "But Vogue might ask us to do an event for them and I won't be able to turn it down,"' says Maria Georgiou, Rhiannon's business partner. 'It's hard to think of the future because, for us, that's constantly changing.'

Gilles has also experienced these more subtle psychological struggles. 'Ego was involved because before, as a graphic designer, I was doing exhibitions, so there's some status involved with that,' he says. 'When you stop that, and when you build up a new idea, it's very crappy for at least two years.'

What he found helpful was simple math, which gave him the confidence that it'd all be worth it in the end and that the pain would eventually subside. 'We calculated how many sales we'd need to have a reasonable lifestyle. It was all calculated,' he says. 'It all boiled down to one number – we need to sell this many tiles every month. Then we'd think: do we think this is feasible? And we really did.'

(PART TWO)

Work-life balance

Mam Sham, run by Maria Georgiou *(top left)* and Rhiannon Butler *(top right)*, works with local chefs and food brands to host supper clubs.

One of the misconceptions about being your own boss is that you'll have more free time. While, yes, you probably won't have anyone to answer to – so you can, in theory, start work at midday or finish early – that's unlikely to be the case in practice.

Many business founders find themselves working harder than they have ever before. They'll often work evenings and weekends, and rarely will they take a holiday. Because there's no set schedule, you have to implement your own boundaries, which isn't easy with the enduring pressure of having to grow a business.

'I think it comes from a fear that maybe the jobs will stop coming – though, of course, that's not rational,' explains Gilles. 'But it's also about wanting to serve. You love what you're doing, so you just add another task to another task and, before you know it, you have a 14-hour day.'

Finding this balance is something he's actively working on, he says. 'We certainly don't romanticize doing 12-hour days. We do them, but we don't like them.' After several years of working around the clock, it's dawned on him that he can't continue at the same pace. 'It's better to have a smaller profit margin and to have more time for yourself,' he says. 'It's an investment in yourself.'

Recently, Gilles has stopped working weekends. 'It always turns out that, in the end, it wasn't needed,' he says. In the evenings, he tries to avoid answering emails. 'Learning that the client always says they're in a hurry, even when they're not in a hurry, is important,' he says.

He also makes sure to carve out time for holidays. 'When [your business is] two people, it can be hard to take time off because you put more workload on the other,' he says. 'But we're realizing that you don't have to feel guilty to go away because you always come back fresher.'

ALWAYS BE FLEXIBLE

In some jobs, like hospitality, the working hours can stretch around the clock. An evening social might be enjoyable, but it's still not personal time. 'When you slip into times when there's less structure, the lines become really blurred,' says Maria of Mam Sham. 'We're living in an age of everything being online and everyone sharing everything about their lives online, so there's a constant panic of being left behind.'

To add some exercise into their routine and to maximize their time outside, Rhiannon and Maria try to walk everywhere, rather than taking

Luke Findlay *(right)* launched Supa Ya Ramen in 2019 as a supper club. The pandemic scuppered his plans to open a permanent site in March 2020, but it finally opened in London's Dalston in 2021.

'It's better to have a smaller profit margin and to have more time for yourself.'

the bus or tube, where they tend to be on their phones or checking emails.

Shivas has also learned the importance of flexibility. He tries to listen to what his body needs to ensure that when he is working, he's doing so efficiently. 'You have a responsibility to yourself and the long-term growth of your business to always get into that mental headspace when you'll do the best work in the most effective time,' he says. 'If that means I go for a two-hour [bike] ride on a Monday afternoon, that's fine; I might not work for the rest of the day but, after dinner, I'm sitting down and working on research.'

At Supa Ya Ramen, Luke has learned that, for him, the easiest route to a work-life balance is building a team that he can rely on. When he opened his first restaurant in 2021, he was able to take weekends and some weeknights off without worrying. 'The opening team in Dalston were amazing,' he recalls. 'I felt relaxed enough that I could start taking time off.'

But, since then, it's been hard to constantly find the right people. With new openings, he finds himself working around the clock. 'I need to know their standards are as good as mine because I don't want the product to suffer,' he says.

According to Maria and Rhiannon, building an audience has also been a crucial part of Mam Sham's success. 'We worked like a thousand jobs in hospitality while we worked on Mam Sham,' Maria says. They decided to go full-time just before the pandemic, and the only reason was because their work with Mam Sham was taking up the vast majority of their time and energy.

'As Mam Sham became busier, it became clear that we [didn't] have time to do that other job,' explains Rhiannon. 'Don't be ashamed of doing stuff on the side,' adds Maria. 'It's a really unfair pressure to decide that you're going to do this thing full-time [while you're] completely panicking about your financial future.'

For Shivas, the process was similar. He quit his job in music management and decided to pursue Friendly Pressure as a full-time project in September 2022. He was optimistic that it would be a viable business based on his Instagram following. 'I started posting things and it quickly blew up,' he says.

But he decided to take the plunge only after selling thousands of pounds worth of speakers to a guy he met in Ibiza. The customer's friend

'You can't just open a shop and expect people to come.'

(**PART THREE**)

Timings

For years before he finally launched Supa Ya Ramen, Luke had ambitions of running his own business. He'd been working in kitchens for decades, and he craved some autonomy. It was really just a question of when.

The answer to that question came to him in 2020, as his supper clubs, which he was hosting at his apartment, became increasingly popular. He was also hosting pop-ups all across London, serving his ramen in Hackney and Fitzrovia, to name just a few areas. Wherever it was, there'd always be a queue.

Slowly, it dawned on him that he had enough of an audience to justify Supa Ya Ramen's first permanent restaurant. 'The original plan was to do a couple of pop-ups and leave it at that,' he says. 'But we had a big following, so we knew we were going to be busy when we opened. This meant we weren't worried about opening the doors and nobody coming.'

TAKE THE LEAP

Millions of people around the world share Luke's ambition and want to set up their own business, but so often they fail to act. One reason is because they worry whether it's the right time.

Unfortunately, there's no one-size-fits-all answer to this question, but there are things you can do to minimize the risk and smooth the transition into life as a business owner. Just like Luke did, for many people it'll be important to first build up an audience.

'Unless you've got loads of money, just plug away at it in your spare evenings and on the weekends,' Luke says. 'You can't just open a shop and expect people to come.'

Friendly Pressure tracks down and sells rare, quality audio equipment, like these speakers from manufacturer JBL, which the brand exported from Japan.

Shivas Howard-Brown
(left) works with
musicians like Errol
Anderson *(right)* of
club-night community
Touching Bass.

then asked Shivas to supply enough custom
speakers to fit out his whole home. 'It was
extremely validating because suddenly all those
sacrifices I'd made made sense,' he recalls. 'If you
don't ever take those risks, then the reward will
never present itself.'

In the end, the decision, he says, was quite
easy. 'I decided to focus on stuff that would excite
me, which is essentially finding really rare,
amazing-looking speakers that are ridiculously
cheap and adding a markup,' he explains. 'Then
I could sustain my lifestyle.'

SPEAK TO OTHERS

Sometimes, says Gilles, you have to just jump on
an opportunity. For years, he and Jaap had been
discussing the idea of setting up a tile company
together. 'That was just all we wanted to do at the
time,' he says. 'Everyone around us thought we
were crazy.' But it never felt like the right time to
pursue it, though, because they were both so busy
– Jaap was refurbishing and selling mid-century
furniture, while Gilles, a freelance graphic
designer, was making experimental designs for
energy-drinks companies. It was only when the
pandemic struck, causing Gilles' work to dry up,
that he realized it was the right moment. 'Within
one week, I didn't have a job any more,' he says.
This ultimately made the risk of setting up
Studio GdB much smaller.

Outside of this, according to Luke, it's
important to do your own research. 'Speak to
people who've done it,' he says. 'A broad spectrum
of people who've done it.' These should be in
different fields, so that you can really understand
what the challenges might be and what to expect
– that'll help to inform your decision.

Before he opened his first Supa Ya Ramen site,
Luke asked his friend over at burger restaurant
Patty&Bun when was the right time to go from
pop-up to permanent. Their advice was simple:
'Do it for as long as you can, until it's too big and
you need to open somewhere.'

'If you don't ever
take those risks,
then the reward
will never
present itself.'

Courier

Jeff Taylor Editor-in-Chief
Cain Fleming Managing Director
Kate McInerney, Lisa Rahman Creative Directors
John Sunyer Editor
Benjamin Chiou Managing Editor
Daniel Giacopelli Editor-at-Large
Michael Downes Finance Director

EDITORIAL
Bre Graham Lifestyle Editor
Karis Hustad News Editor
Caspar Barnes Junior Reporter
Bhavini Patadia Editorial Assistant

Lola Oduba Chief Sub-Editor
Lauren Bowes Sub-Editor

STUDIO
Charlotte Matters Senior Art Director
Anna Jay Photography Director
Sara Taglioretti Photo Editor
Sean Thomas Designer
Sureeyah Grant Digital Content Manager

Abby Draycott Senior Production Manager
Ida Jankowska Production Assistant

CLIENT SERVICES AND OPERATIONS
Maverick Pettit-Taylor Distribution Manager
Julia Ahern Marketing & Communications Manager
Laura Raimondi Brand Partnerships Executive
Sam Moreton Financial Analyst
Evan Blanque Office Manager

CONTRIBUTING WORDS
Megan Carnegie, Louis Cheslaw, Clare Finney,
Danielle Han, Will Higginbotham, William Ralston,
Madeleine Rothery, Pam Vivatsurakit

CONTRIBUTING DESIGN
Tim George, Mark Leeds

Typefaces used Sharp Sans, GT Alpina, Atlas

Printed by Printer Trento S.r.l., Trento

Made in Europe.

Published by gestalten, Berlin 2023
ISBN: 978-3-96704-111-8
© Die Gestalten Verlag GmbH & Co. KG, Berlin 2023

For more information, and to order books,
please visit www.gestalten.com

Bibliographic information published by the Deutsche
Nationalbibliothek. The Deutsche Nationalbibliothek lists
this publication in the Deutsche Nationalbibliografie;
detailed bibliographic data is available online at www.dnb.de

This book was printed on paper certified according to the
standards of the FSC®.

PHOTOGRAPHY
On the cover
Amy and Kiddo Cosio are the founders of El Union in San Juan, on the
north-west coast of the Philippines. Since opening in 2013, El Union has
grown from a stripped-back coffee shack to a community hub complete
with a skating bowl and bean roastery. Unsurprisingly, the couple kickstart
every working day with a cup of coffee. Photographed by **Jilson Tiu**

Inside
MOND by **Ryan Wijayaratne**
CLÉMENT BOUTEILLE FLEURS, WANG & SÖDERSTRÖM by **Luke & Nik**
EL UNION by **Sonny Thakur**
OLO SURF & NATURE by **Poppy Thorpe**
LAURENCEAIRLINE by **Nuits Balnéaires**
CASA ETÉREA by **Pia Riverola**
PNY by **Thomas Chéné**
CAMP YOSHI by **Dorothy Wang**
CITIZEN OF NOWHERE, SUNNE VOYAGE by **Natthawut Taeja**
MØRNING.FYI AND FERAL by **Max Miechowski**
CASA LAWA by **Carmen Colombo**
TREVAREFABRIKKEN by **Elin Fröderberg**
MIRAI by **Sage Brown**
COYOL RESTAURANT by **Paz Howell, Jessica Last and Charlie Wild**
ŌSHADI by **Ashish Chandra and Manou**
TRUCK by **Mitsuru Wakabayashi**
OLI DE L'OLIVETA by **Coke Bartrina**
LA BANCHINA by **Sam A. Harris**
SENSE OF SELF by **Abigail Varney**
AGUA MÁGICA by **Enrique Leyva**
OLD CARPET FACTORY by **Marco Argüello**

CONTRIBUTING PHOTOGRAPHERS
**James Anastasi, Marco Argüello, Joseph Beeching, Kate Berry, Serena
Brown, Marc Krause, Puzzleman Leung, Michelle Mishina, Tracy Nguyen,
Nikki To, Nikola Tomevski, Caroline Tompkins, Mariam Wo Ching**